Stitch Along

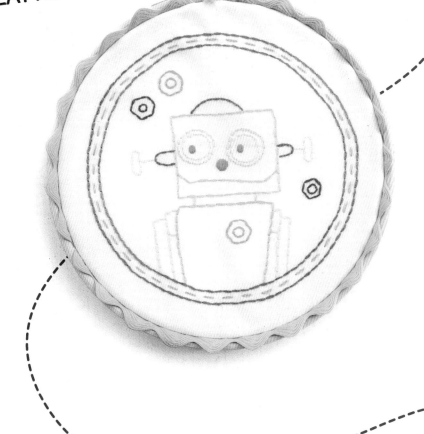

An Imprint of Sterling Publishing
387 Park Avenue South
New York, NY 10016

ISBN 978-1-4547-0786-8

Doh, Jenny.
  Stitch along : 10 stitchers, 30 projects, 100 embroidery motifs / Jenny Doh.
      pages cm
  Includes index.
  ISBN 978-1-4547-0786-8
  1. Embroidery--Patterns. I. Title.
  TT770.5.D64 2014
  746.44--dc23
                                        2013037456

Distributed in Canada by Sterling Publishing
c/o Canadian Manda Group, 165 Dufferin Street
Toronto, Ontario, Canada M6K 3H6
Distributed in the United Kingdom by GMC Distribution Services
Castle Place, 166 High Street, Lewes, East Sussex, England BN7 1XU
Distributed in Australia by Capricorn Link (Australia) Pty. Ltd.
P.O. Box 704, Windsor, NSW 2756, Australia

For information about custom editions, special sales, and premium and corporate purchases, please contact Sterling Special Sales at 800-805-5489 or specialsales@sterlingpublishing.com.

Email academic@larkbooks.com for information about desk and examination copies.
The complete policy can be found at larkcrafts.com.

Manufactured in China

2 4 6 8 10 9 7 5 3 1

larkcrafts.com

Stitch Along

10 stitchers, 30 projects, 100 embroidery motifs

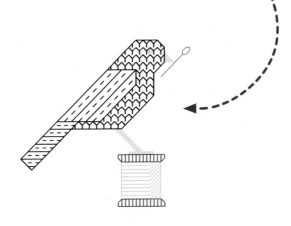

Jenny Doh

LARK

Contents

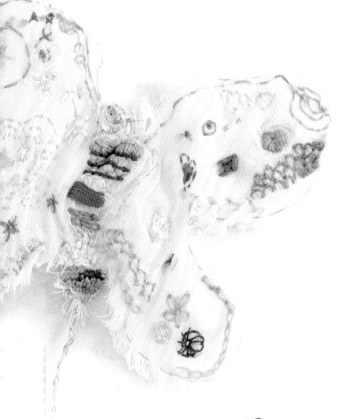

Basics

There is magic in a simple strand of thread and a needle. With pattern motifs or your own imagination, you can create scenes and pictures on fabric that are sure to charm and delight. While embroidery is a timeless art that has been around for centuries, stitching with modern colors and patterns allows this classic art form to be contemporary and fun. Before we dive into the projects presented by the talented artists in this book, let's go over the basic techniques, tools, and materials you'll need to get started.

tools and materials

Start gathering your tools and materials by collecting the items in the Stitching Tool Kit (see page 8), and we'll talk through details on the following pages.

FLOSS AND THREAD

Most of the projects in this book use six-strand embroidery floss. Standard embroidery floss is made of cotton, but it also comes in metallic, silk, and linen. Floss comes in a wide variety of colors for all your project needs, and it's sold in little bundles, called skeins.

Each skein is made up of six strands wrapped together. For projects where you'd like a thicker embroidered line, you can keep all six strands intact. If you want a thinner line, you can easily pull the strands apart and use however many you'd like. You can even use just one strand and hand-sew fabric pieces together. For the projects in this book that use six-strand floss, we will note how many strands are used in each project. We will also note the color and the DMC color code if available. DMC is a popular brand of floss that many embroidery designers use.

Though the most common stitching medium is embroidery floss, you can use any sort of thread. Perle cotton is another popular choice. Perle cotton isn't meant to be unraveled, so select your desired thicknesses from the start. Perle cotton comes in skeins or balls, in assorted thicknesses. The smaller the size number, the thicker the cotton, and vice versa. Yarn is another great choice for embroidery, as long as you choose one that is smooth enough to go through your desired material.

STITCHING TOOL KIT

Each project will specify the color and number of strands of embroidery floss or other thread used. In addition, most projects will use the following materials, so have them on hand before you begin.

Scissors
Needles
Iron and ironing board
Nonpermanent
 fabric marker
Embroidery hoop
Tweezers
Straight pins
Thimble
Transferring tools (optional)*
 ▸ **Laser copier**
 ▸ **Cellophane tape**
 ▸ **Light table or good**
  source of light
 ▸ **Lead pencil**
 ▸ **Carbon paper**
 ▸ **Stylus**
 ▸ **Thin tissue paper**

* Depending on which transferring method you use (see Transferring Your Motif, page 10), these are the transfer tools you'll want to have on hand.

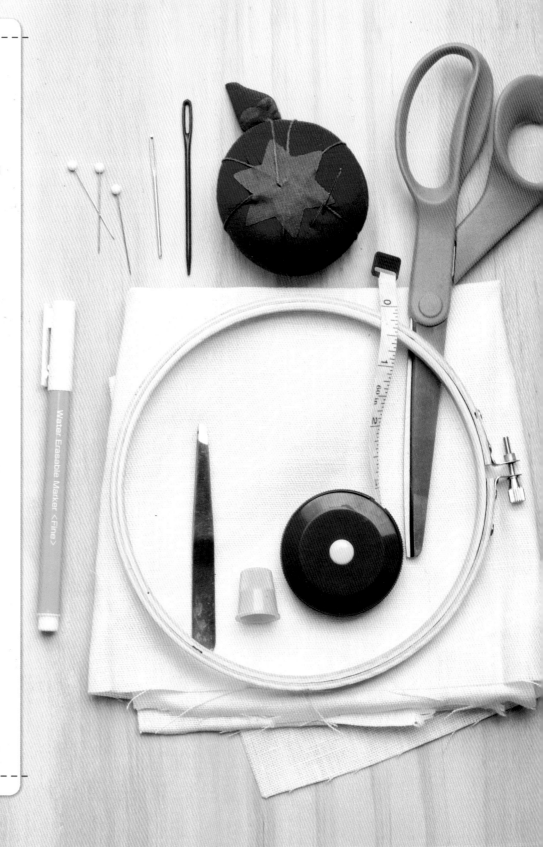

NEEDLES

There are many types and sizes of needles out there, and you are encouraged to experiment (A). The longer embroidery needles usually have a larger eye (hole), and a lower number size. For example, a #1 needle is longer than a #10.

The bottom line: Any needle will do, as long as the eye is large enough to thread the floss or thread you are working with, and the point is sharp enough to comfortably pierce through your fabric. The projects in this book do not specify needle size because needle selection is not an exact science. Also, since needles don't come with sizes marked on them, it's easy to forget precisely what size they are—sometimes even the packaging doesn't specify needle size. Keep a good variety of needles in a pincushion for convenience.

If you use yarn to embroider, you'll want to use a larger yarn needle (either plastic or metal) for ease in threading (B).

EMBROIDERY HOOP

An embroidery hoop holds your projects in place while you're stitching. While it's possible to stitch without one, using a hoop will tighten your fabrics for a smooth surface and decrease the amount of puckering caused when pulling stitches. Embroidery hoops come in plastic or wood; while wood is traditional, plastic hoops last longer and are sturdier. Hoops come in a variety of sizes. If you're just starting out, a 6-inch (15.2 cm) hoop is a great investment and will work for a majority of the projects in this book. The great thing about hoops is that if your finished project is going to be bigger than 6 inches (15.2 cm), you can just readjust the hoop as you move from section to section (C).

FABRIC

You can embroider on any fabric you'd like, and you really don't even have to limit yourself to fabric. As long as a needle can go through it, you can embroider it! Quilter's cotton, canvas, satin, and denim are all great substrates for embroidery, which means you can easily add stitching to canvas totes, jeans, and kitchen towels. If you'd like to embroider on more delicate fabrics, such as silk or thin cotton, add a stabilizer to the back of the fabric before stitching (see page 11). But as long as you have a sturdy embroidery hoop, an added stabilizer won't be necessary, especially for the projects in this book.

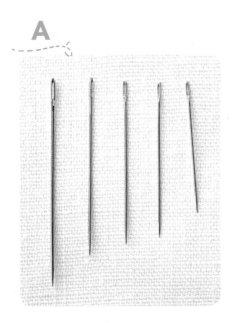

A

B

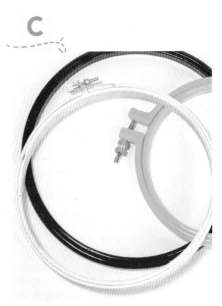

C

stitching technique

Now that we've covered the tools and materials, it's time to talk about the embroidery process. Put simply, here's the order of events:

1 Choose a motif.

2 Transfer the motif to your fabric.

3 Add stabilizer if necessary.

4 Stretch the fabric onto the hoop and secure it.

5 Thread the needle and stitch away!

6 Remove transfer lines.

7 Finish the project.

CHOOSING A MOTIF

The motifs seen in each project are provided alongside the instructions and photos. You will want to copy the images, resize them as needed, and transfer them to the fabric. Depending on your method of transfer, you may need to reverse your images before printing so they don't come out backwards in the end.

TRANSFERRING YOUR MOTIF

There are several ways you can transfer your chosen motif to your fabric. The assorted methods work differently with various fabrics, so play around until you determine your preference and the best option for the specific project.

iron-on transfers

The iron-on transfer method begins with making a laser photocopy or print of the motif onto transfer paper. Before printing, reverse the image in an image-editing program. Then place the print facedown on the fabric and apply heat with an iron. The lines will transfer from the print onto the fabric and will be permanent, so you'll need to cover the entire motif with stitches. This method works especially well with intricate motifs that may include thin lines or text.

tracing method

For the tracing method, you'll need a nonpermanent fabric marker and a good source of light—either a brightly lit window or a light table. Tape the printed motif onto the table or window, then place the fabric over the motif and trace it using the marker. Once you are finished with the embroidery, the marker will wash off easily with water. This method is ideal for lighter fabrics and patterns where you don't want to have to worry about covering every part of the traced motif with stitches.

You can also use a lead pencil to trace the motif onto your fabric. The pencil won't be permanent, but it will be harder to remove than the nonpermanent fabric marker, so be sure to cover the pencil with your stitches if you go this route.

carbon paper method

If fabric markers or pencils don't show up on your fabric, carbon paper is another way to transfer a motif. Carbon paper comes in a variety of colors, so pick one that contrasts with the fabric you're using. Lay your fabric down on a hard surface, followed by a piece of carbon paper, and then the printed motif. Trace the pattern with a blunt object, such as a dull pencil or stylus and check that the lines are showing up on the fabric.

tissue paper method

In the tissue paper method, trace your motif onto thin tissue paper, then pin the tissue paper to your fabric. Stitch through the paper and fabric. When you're finished, you can rip the tissue paper away from the fabric. Use a needle or tweezers to catch the little edges of paper that may be stuck underneath the stitches.

ADDING FABRIC STABILIZER

If you're working with a delicate fabric, you can add a sheet of fabric stabilizer to the back of the fabric to strengthen it. You can use a sheet of water-soluble stabilizer (recommended for delicate fabrics) or a sheet with adhesive on one side and tear-away paper on the other. Following the manufacturer's instructions, cut the stabilizer to fit the area where you'll be stitching, adhere it to the back of the fabric, and then proceed to stitch through both the fabric and the stabilizer. When you're finished, you can rinse or tear away the parts that aren't stitched down. A pair of tweezers may be helpful to reach the intricate areas.

PUTTING FABRIC ON THE HOOP

Once your fabric is ready with a traced motif and stabilizer, if necessary, it's time to add the hoop. Lay the inside hoop down on a flat surface, then lay the fabric down with the traced motif in the center of the hoop. Then lay the outside hoop on top of the fabric. Fit the hoops together and tighten the screw to secure, pulling the fabric as you tighten so the area to be stitched is nice and taut.

THREADING AND STITCHING

Start by cutting a length of floss in your chosen color. Thread your needle with one end and tie a knot in the opposite end. Now you're ready to go.

Each project includes a list of stitches used. If you're just starting out, this will allow you to choose projects you're comfortable with as you're learning. Next, look at the stitch guide—a diagram that illustrates which stitches are used and where. Compare this to the photograph of the finished project to get an idea of what you will be stitching.

Begin by bringing your needle up from the back to the front into your motif, so the knot catches on the back of the embroidered piece. Follow the stitch guide, taking your time to work through the different stitches and colors. You can choose to approach the project by color or by section. Approaching by color means you complete all stitches of one color before moving on to the next color. Approaching by section means you complete all stitches in one section before moving on to a different area.

When you come to the end of your length of floss, or if you're at the end of a line or color, bring your needle through to the back of your piece, then thread the needle under a stitch and tie a knot around it. Cut off the extra floss and rethread your needle.

REMOVING TRANSFER LINES

Once your embroidery design is finished, remove it from the hoop. At this point, if you used a nonpermanent fabric marker to trace the motif, gently rinse it out with water. You may need to rub a small amount of a gentle detergent between your fingers, but the marker should come out without any problems. Lay the fabric flat to dry.

FINISHING THE EMBROIDERY

Once your piece is nearly dry, lay it facedown on a towel. Apply heat with an iron to remove any wrinkles in the fabric or stitches. Some of the projects in this book include steps beyond finishing the embroidery, such as sewing, but these will be explained in detail within the projects.

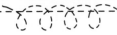

HOMEMADE BINDING

Binding can be purchased in stores, but you can make your own with your favorite fabric. Here's how.

1 Determine the length of the binding you will need by adding together the lengths of the edges you are binding, plus an additional few inches.

2 Cut strips of fabric to the desired width. Connect the strips as needed to make one continuous strip in one of the following ways:
- ▶ Pin and stitch the short ends of the strips together (A), with right sides facing. Press seams open.
- ▶ Pin the short ends of your strips together at a right angle, with right sides facing, and stitch diagonally across the corner (B). Trim the seam allowance, and press seams open.

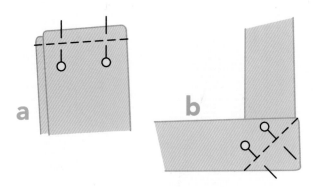

THE TIES THAT BIND

Making mitered corners with bias binding is easier than you think! It requires two easy folds at every corner. There are two projects in this book that involve binding: the Blackbird Sewing Kit (page 71) and the Dinkie Birdie Art Quilt (page 118).

1 Lay your project flat on your work surface and trim the layers so they are all the same size.

2 Starting midway on one edge or near a corner, pin the right side of the binding to the right side of the fabric, folding the starting edge to the wrong side.

3 Stitch to the first corner, making sure to backstitch for reinforcement before you clip the threads to remove the project from the machine. Fold the binding straight up over itself to form a 45° angle at the corner (C).

4 Fold the binding straight down to make it even with the next edge and continue pinning and stitching the binding in place (D). Continue working your way around the edges, using the same process for additional corners.

5 When you are near your starting point, stitch your binding strip over the folded-over starting edge of the binding.

6 Fold the binding over the edges to the back. Make sure that the folded edge of the binding on the back side covers the seam line that attached the binding and pin it down along the edges. Create diagonal folds at the corners and pin.

7 Working from the back, use a slip stitch to attach the binding.

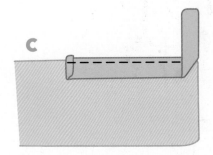

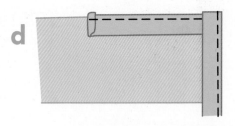

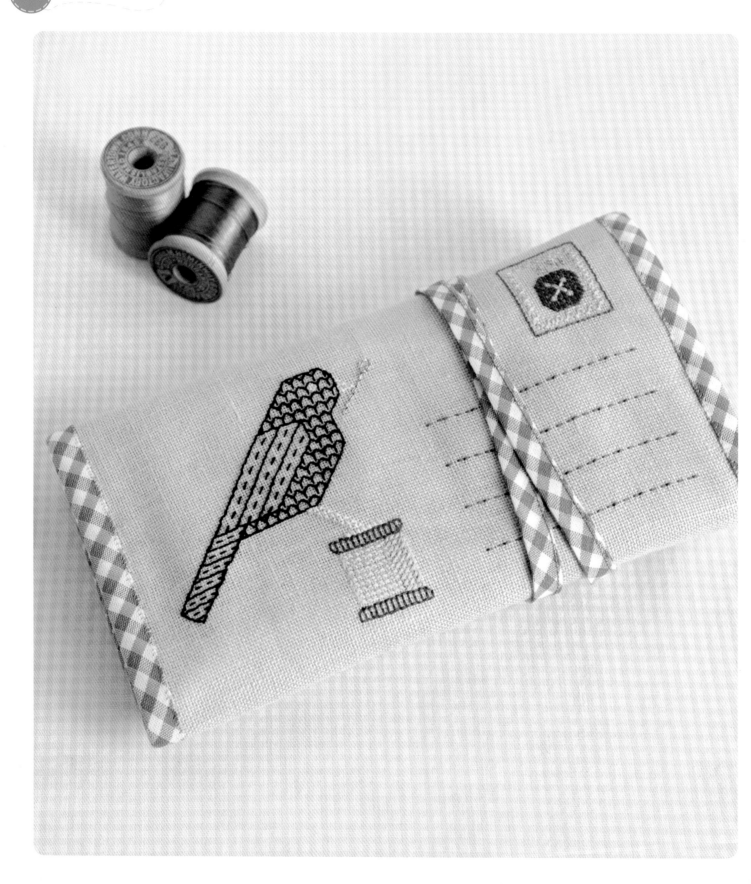

stitch library

Over the next few pages, you'll see several of the basic stitches that will be used in the projects in this book.

BACK STITCH

The back stitch is a great stitch to use for outlining, because there are no spaces between the stitches. Make a straight stitch, then start the next stitch a short distance away and stitch back to directly in front of the first stitch.

BASKETWEAVE STITCH

Make a row of straight stitches of equal lengths leaving some space between them. Make a second row of straight stitches tucked in between the first row of stitches, offsetting them a bit.

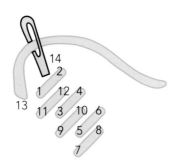

BASKETWEAVE SATIN STITCH

Make groups of three or four stitches in alternating horizontal and vertical blocks.

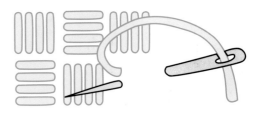

BLANKET STITCH
(also known as Buttonhole Stitch)

You've probably seen this decorative stitch along the edge of a blanket. As you make parallel straight stitches, catch the lower loop of floss or thread as shown.

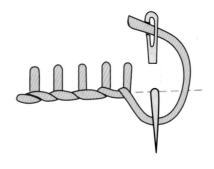

BULLION STITCH

Similar to the French knot, pull the needle up at point A, down at B, then up at C, though don't pull the needle all the way through yet. Wrap the thread around the needle several times and then pull the needle up from C while holding the wound thread close to the surface of the fabric with your thumb. Pull the needle down through point B.

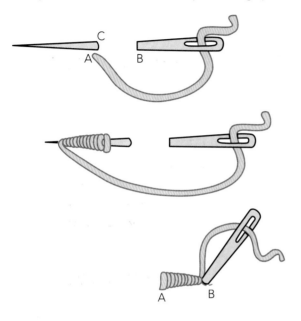

CHAIN STITCH

Pull the needle up through the back, then put the needle back in through the same point until you have a loop of floss on the front. Bring the needle back up through the loop, then continue to make small loops to form a chain. At the end of a chain row, make a small stitch over the last loop to secure it. Position the chain stitches in a zigzag formation to create a zigzag chain stitch.

CLOSED BLANKET STITCH
(also known as Closed Buttonhole Stitch)

Bring needle up at A, down at B, then up at C, making sure you catch the thread so that it creates a diagonal slant. Bring needle down at D, up at E, making sure the thread is behind the needle. Bring the needle back down at D and up through F, making sure the thread is behind the needle.

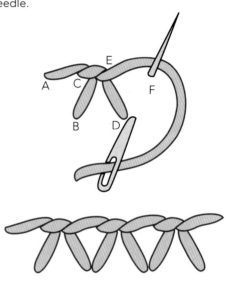

COUCHING STITCH

Lay down the first thread and with the second thread, secure it down at even intervals with tiny straight stitches worked over the top.

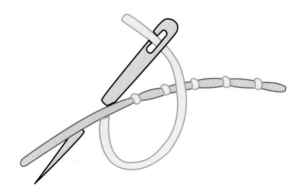

EYELET WHEEL

Bring the needle up at A, down at B, up at A again, and down at C. To start the next stitch, come up at D.

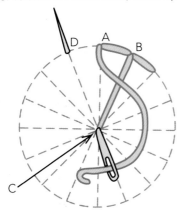

FEATHER STITCH

Make a loose, diagonal straight stitch. Push the needle back up through the fabric at a point close to where the first stitch ended, and catch the first stitch as you secure the second stitch. Continue in this manner, but alternate the direction of the diagonal.

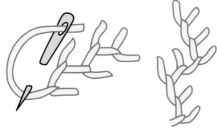

FLY STITCH

Make a loose straight stitch horizontally, leaving a slight loop. Hold the loop down with your fingers, and push the needle back up through the fabric in the middle of the loop. Catch the loop in the stitch, and push the needle back through the fabric.

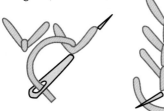

FRENCH KNOT

Bring the needle up through the fabric, wrap the floss around the needle, and push the needle back through the fabric close to the first stitch point. Pull the needle tightly to close up the stitch.

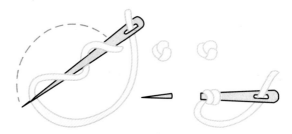

HERRINGBONE STITCH

Herringbone stitches are similar in action to the cross stitch, but instead of making the X's perfect, you make one side of the X much larger than the other side. All in a row, the irregular X's look like a herringbone pattern.

LAZY DAISY STITCH

Bring the needle up at A then back down close to A, but not all the way through, making a loop. Bring needle up at B and down at C.

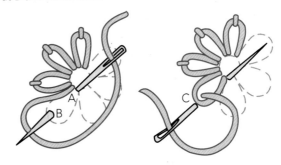

LONG AND SHORT STITCH

Make a straight stitch, then make a second straight stitch beside it that's half the size. Continue alternating between shorter and longer stitches. This stitch easily fills a large area with one color.

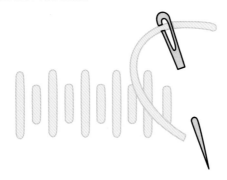

OPEN CRETAN

Bring the needle up at A, down at B, then up at C. Bring the needle down at D, then up at E.

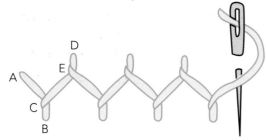

PETAL STITCH

Bring the needle up at A, down at B, and up at C. Bring the needle down right next to C and up at D, making sure thread is behind needle. Bring needle down at E, and up at F.

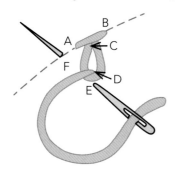

SATIN STITCH

Satin stitches are another way to fill in an area with color. Make a straight stitch, then make a second straight stitch directly next to it, a little longer or shorter as needed. Continue making stitches side by side to fill your intended space.

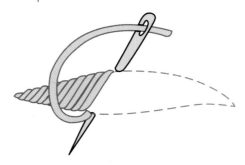

SCALLOP STITCH

The scallop stitch is very similar to the Lazy Daisy, but the loops are shorter and wider, and made in a line rather than a circle.

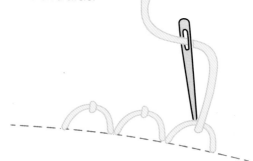

SPLIT STITCH

Begin the split stitch by making one straight stitch. Then bring the needle up through the middle of the first stitch, splitting it in half. Continue making stitches and splitting them in half for a continuous line.

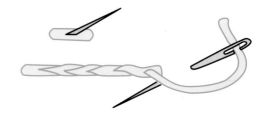

STAR STITCH

One way to make a star stitch is to start with a cross stitch (see page 20), and then add two straight stitches in a plus sign (+) on top. Another way is to make a long-armed X and add one straight stitch across (see page 36).

STEM STITCH

This stitch works well in making curved lines, like stems! Make a straight stitch, and then make another next to it, starting near the middle of the first stitch to offset the second stitch. Pull it tight and repeat the stitch.

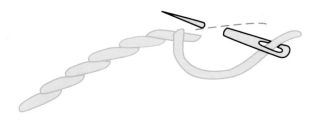

STRAIGHT STITCH
(also known as Running Stitch and Seed Stitch)

Push the needle up through the fabric at one point and down at another point. This is the most basic and versatile of embroidery stitches. You can make the stitches very small to look like dots or seeds, or you can make long dashes. Stitch in a straight line or in a variety of clusters to create small designs such as flowers and stars.

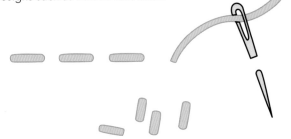

THREADED RUNNING STITCH
(also known as Holbein Stitch)

Make a line of straight stitches that look like evenly spaced dashes. With a second floss strand, weave the needle through the stitches on the front side of the design, going up through one stitch and down through another.

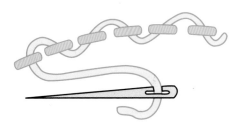

WOVEN ROSE
(also known as Woven Spider Web)

Create a five-point star with five long straight stitches that meet at the center point of the star. With a second thread, start from the center point and weave it above and below the five long stitches in a circular fashion until you reach the end points of the long stitches.

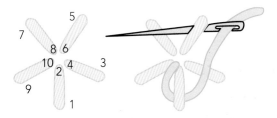

CROSS STITCH BASICS

Cross stitch is a type of embroidery based on an X-shaped stitch. To begin, make a waste knot by making a knot and pushing the needle from the front side of the aida cloth (see next page) or other fabric to the back side, several squares away from the center of the cloth. Pull the needle up at the first square, and as you continue making your stitches, do it so that the length of the floss from the knot to the first stitch gets securely covered with the back-and-forth stitches. Snip the waste knot and discard.

To make a full cross stitch:

1 Locate the square on the aida cloth where you will make the cross stitch and pull the needle from the back side to the front side of the cloth through the hole at the lower right corner of the square.

2 Push the needle back down from front to back through the hole at the upper left corner of the square.

3 Pull the needle from the back to front through the hole at the lower left corner of the square.

4 Push the needle back down from front to back through the hole at the upper right corner of the square.

To make a three-quarter cross stitch:

1 Repeat step 1 from the full cross stitch instructions.

2 Push the needle back down from front to back through the very middle of the square to make a quarter stitch. Note: There is no hole in the middle of the square so you will need to pierce the cloth carefully.

3 Repeat steps 3 and 4 from the full cross stitch instructions.

4 To finish, weave the floss in and out of some of the stitches on the back side of the aida and snip.

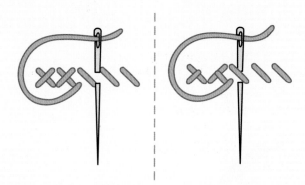

CROSS STITCH TIPS

▶ Find the center of the aida cloth (see next page) or other fabric by folding it in half from top to bottom and then from left to right. Always start embroidering from the center point.

▶ Approach the embroidery by color so that within a section that you are working on, you complete all stitches of one color before moving to the next color.

▶ When you come to the end of your length of floss or at the end of a section of color, bring your needle through to the back of your piece and weave it behind the stitches you have made. Leave a tail approximately 1 inch (1.3 cm) long on the back and stitch over this tail as you continue to stitch your design.

▶ The three-quarter cross stitch is a variation derived from the full cross stitch. You can make other variations (as seen in Sami Teasdale's projects, pages 71 to 78) by making stitches based on counted squares.

UNDERSTANDING AIDA CLOTH AND WASTE AIDA

Aida cloth is the traditional substrate for cross stitch embroidery. Waste aida helps guide cross stitch embroidery when stitching on non-aida cloth.

Aida cloth is a fairly stiff open-weave mesh fabric. The number of squares per square inch of the fabric is what determines the size of the cloth. For example, a 10-count aida cloth has 10 x 10 squares per square inch, while 16-count aida cloth has 16 x 16 squares per square inch. The higher the count, the smaller the squares on the cloth. Each square has four distinct holes that the needle can pass through.

Motifs for cross stitch are designed on 10 x 10 square grids. Therefore, rather than transferring a motif onto aida cloth, stitchers read the grid-based designs while counting and embroidering the design (based on the small squares) onto the aida cloth.

Waste aida looks like regular aida—designed as an open-weave fabric manufactured with a certain number of squares per inch, with holes at each corner of each square. Pin the waste aida onto the fabric you would like to embroider and either pin or hand-baste the layers together. Use the waste aida as an embroidery guide; then, after you finish stitching, dampen the waste aida and remove it with the help of tweezers.

Evenweave linen fabrics are also popular choices for counted cross stitch since the loose weave allows you to count squares with four distinct points.

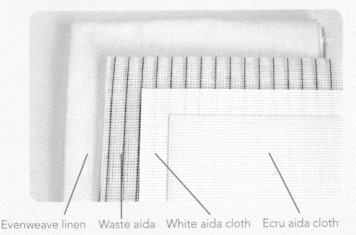

Evenweave linen Waste aida White aida cloth Ecru aida cloth

A FEW FINAL NOTES

There are a few terms and methods that you'll see mentioned in some of the projects that we want to make sure you are aware of.

True Up: Occasionally, instructions will ask you to true up the fabric. This means to make a piece of fabric or layers of fabric balanced, straight, and true to grain by cutting or ripping the thickness(es).

Fill Stitch: Instructions will at times refer to fill stitching, which is a process of filling in an area, like a leaf, with stitches—similar to coloring a shape in with a crayon. Satin stitches and long and short stitches are two that are frequently used to fill-stitch. However, any stitch can become a fill stitch, as long as it is repeated within the section to fill up that space.

Free-Motion Stitching: In several projects, you will be asked to use your sewing machine to incorporate free-motion stitching. To do so, drop the feed dogs on your machine, and attach a darning foot (or quilting foot). In regular sewing, the feed dogs grip and guide the fabric while you sew. Because the feed dogs are lowered in free-motion stitching, the fabric is loose and free to move the way you want it to move as you guide it through the machine to create freeform stitch lines.

pretty flowers stitch along with *Charlotte Lyons*

photo: Becky Novacek

charlotte's stitches are full of personality

I love Charlotte's ability to blend vintage fabrics (as well as vintage-inspired fabrics like her Tilly line for Blend fabrics) with modern stitch patterns. Not only is she repurposing, but she's also creating a charming, homespun look that warms up any corner of a room. Charlotte's projects are sweet, simple, and full of personality. Stitch along with Charlotte to learn how to apply darling patterns to your own favorite vintage fabrics.

— Jenny Doh

Question: What inspires you about stitching?
CL: I am inspired by the whole process from designing to making thread and stitch choices. My crafting roots are in stitching. My mother stitched and so did my grandmother and probably hers as well. It's an ancient cross-cultural craft that is easy to learn, with materials that are simple.

Question: What materials do you typically stitch on?
CL: I like to repurpose materials, and I often use them in my stitched projects. I'll either stitch solely on a vintage napkin or cloth, or I'll combine old and new fabrics into a sort of collage. Then I'll stitch on top to secure all the layers and add color and interest.

Question: What do you enjoy most about stitching?
CL: I enjoy the peacefulness of the craft as well as playing with different stitches, colors, and forms to create pictures with thread. There are endless combinations to try and I like the challenge of making those small decisions along the way. Adding words or initials personalizes the finished piece in a meaningful way.

Embroidered Zipcase

Zipcases are addictive!
Prepare several
embroidered strips
following the steps here,
and then sew them in
assembly line fashion
to give as gifts to your
special friends.

STITCH ALONG

1 Size the motif (next page) to measure approximately 10 x 2 inches (25.4 x 5.1 cm).

2 Transfer the motif (see page 10) onto the front of the linen strip.

3 Loosely baste the linen strip onto the slightly larger piece of muslin. Secure the fabrics in an embroidery hoop and embroider through both fabric layers according to the stitch guide with cream perle cotton.

4 Take the finished piece out of the hoop and remove any transfer lines as needed (see page 12). True up the muslin to the size of the linen strip.

SEW ALONG

1 Assemble the front of the case:
  ▶ Pin a strip of rickrack along the right side top edge of the embroidered strip with the center of the rickrack ½ inch (1.3 mm) from the raw edge. Machine-baste in place down the center of the rickrack.
  ▶ Pin the brown patterned quilting cotton (top front) on top of the rickrack, right sides facing and aligned with the embroidered top edge.
  ▶ From the wrong side of the embroidered piece,

machine-stitch directly over the basting stitch through all thicknesses. Open and press.
  ▶ Attach the remaining rickrack to the opposite long edge of the embroidered strip in the same way, then attach the yellow patterned quilting cotton (bottom front). Open and press.

2 Following the manufacturer's instructions, press a piece of fusible webbing to the wrong side of the assembled front. Then press the remaining piece of fusible webbing to the fabric for the back of the case. True up the two fused pieces to make sure that they are the same size.

3 Replace the standard foot with the zipper foot on your sewing machine and install the zipper as follows:
  ▶ With right sides facing, pin one long side of the zipper to the top edge of the front piece. Stitch in place, removing pins as you go.
  ▶ Pin one of the lining pieces on top, with the right side of the lining facing the wrong side of the zipper. Stitch along the top edge directly over the first stitch line, removing pins as you go.

GATHER UP

Stitching Tool Kit (page 8)
Embroidered Zipcase motif (next page)
1 strip of linen, 11 x 3 inches (27.9 x 7.6 cm)
1 strip of muslin, 12 x 4 inches (30.5 x 10.2 cm)
Two 11-inch (27.9 cm) pieces of rickrack, ⅝ inch (1.6 cm) wide
Sewing machine with standard foot and zipper foot
1 strip of brown patterned quilting cotton (top front), 11 x 2 inches (27.9 x 5.1 cm)
1 piece of yellow patterned quilting cotton (bottom front), 11 x 5 inches (27.9 x 12.7 cm)
2 pieces of fusible webbing, 11 x 8 inches (27.9 x 20.3 cm)
1 piece of fabric for the back, 11 x 8 inches (27.9 x 20.3 cm)
2 pieces of lining fabric, 11 x 8 inches (27.9 x 20.3 cm)
Zipper, 11 inches (27.9 cm) long
1 skein of perle cotton (size 8), cream

Finished dimensions: 10 x 7 inches (24.4 x 17.8 cm)

Seam allowance: ½ inch (1.3 mm)

STITCHES YOU'LL USE

Back stitch
Blanket stitch (also known as Buttonhole stitch)
Chain stitch
Cross stitch (see page 20)
Feather stitch
French knot
Lazy daisy stitch
Satin stitch
Star stitch
Stem stitch
Straight stitch (also known as Running stitch and Seed stitch)

- Press the seam and pull the lining up and over so that the wrong sides of the fabric are facing, and the nonstitched edge of the zipper is at the top.
- Attach the back fabric and lining in the same way to the opposite side of the zipper, making sure the lining fabrics will be facing each other on both sides of the zipper when turned right side out. Press as before. Replace the zipper foot with the standard foot on your sewing machine.

4 Stitch the sides of the bag:
- Place the stitched case on your work surface, with the zipper in the middle (running top to bottom) and the right sides of the front/back piece and the linings facing.

- Pin around the edges and open the zipper.
- Stitch on all sides, leaving a 4-inch (10.2 cm) opening on the bottom edge of the lining layers.

5 Turn the bag right side out through the opening. Whipstitch the opening closed. Push the lining into the bag.

Charlotte Says

- Make the zipcase bigger or smaller depending on your preference.
- Add a wristlet carry strap.
- Add your initials to the stitch design.

Embroidered Zipcase Motif

enlarge 150%

Blanket Stitch
Straight Stitch
Chain Stitch
Star Stitch
Running Stitch
Chain Stitch
Stem Stitch
Straight Stitch
Blanket Stitch
Cross Stitch
Blanket Stitch
Satin Stitch
Chain Stitch

Star Stitch
Back Stitch
Blanket Stitch
Straight Stitch
Chain Stitch
French Knots
Chain Stitch
Stem Stitch
Running Stitch
Lazy Daisy Stitch
Feather Stitch
Running Stitch
Straight Stitch

GATHER UP

Stitching Tool Kit (page 8)

Patchwork Wall Pocket motif (page 29)

Assorted stash fabric for the patchwork front*

Fabric spray adhesive

1 piece of linen for front embroidery: 7½ x 3½ inches (19 x 8.9 cm)

1 piece of muslin (backing for front patchwork), 12 x 9 inches (30.5 x 22.9 cm)

Sewing machine with standard foot and darning foot

1 strip of patterned quilting cotton for top edge, 12 x 1½ inches (30.5 x 3.8 cm)

Perle cotton (size 8), 1 skein each of green, dark yellow, coral, peach, light blue, and dark blue

1 piece of fabric for the back, 12 x 9 inches (30.5 x 22.9 cm)

2 pieces of lining fabric, 12 x 9 inches (30.5 x 22.9 cm)

Stiff cardboard, 10½ x 7½ inches (26.7 x 19 cm)

1 strip of patterned quilting cotton for the strap, 1 x 11 inches (2.5 x 27.9 cm)

Assorted vintage lace, doily, and fabric scraps

Patterned cross-stitch fabric pieces, embellished with touches of cross stitches, add a whole new flavor to the project. If you do not have fabric with a cross-stitch pattern printed on it, you can still embellish patterned fabric with freehand embroidery stitches that complement the design of the fabric.

Finished dimensions: 11 x 8½ inches (27.9 x 21.6 cm)

Seam allowance: ½ inch (1.3 mm)

STITCHES YOU'LL USE

Chain stitch

Cross stitch (see page 20)

French knot

Long and short stitch

Satin stitch

Straight stitch (also known as Running stitch and Seed stitch)

Patchwork Wall Pocket

This patchwork collage method is fun and easy to make, with a muslin base that keeps the boundaries visible and the shape defined. The end result is something pretty, very sturdy, and ready to use.

STITCH AND SEW ALONG

1 With assorted colors of perle cotton, add a few freehand cross stitches to patterned fabric pieces (see Cross Stitch Basics, page 20).

2 Assemble the patchwork front:
  ▸ Spray the back side of the linen piece with fabric spray adhesive and place it on the upper right corner of the muslin backing.

▸ Spray the back side of the cross-stitched pieces with fabric spray adhesive. Make a fabric collage on the muslin piece, allowing some fabrics to overlap. Allow some raw edges to show and/or fold under some edges.

▸ Make sure to allow some patchwork to align with the edges of the muslin, so that when you stitch the sides, the patchwork edge is neatly stitched into the seam.

3 Prepare your sewing machine for free motion stitching by lowering its feed dogs and attaching the darning foot. Free-motion-stitch the edges of these fabric pieces so that they are secured onto the muslin. Replace the darning foot with a standard foot.

4 With right sides facing, pin the strip of quilting cotton along the top edge of the patchwork front and stitch in place. Press this top edge up, away from the main body. Add blanket stitches along the front seam with light blue perle cotton, working through all thicknesses.

5 Size the motif (next page) to measure approximately 6½ x 2 inches (16.5 x 5.1 cm).

6 Transfer the motif (see page 10) onto the center front of the linen patchwork piece.

7 Secure the patchwork in an embroidery hoop and embroider according to the stitch guide. Add a horizontal line of back stitches at the bottom edge and a vertical

row of back stitches at the right side edge with dark blue perle cotton.

8 Take the patchwork fabric out of the hoop and remove any transfer lines as needed (see page 12).

9 Assemble the pieces:
- Lay out the fabric for the back and pin the patchwork piece to it, right sides facing and all edges aligned. Machine-stitch around the two short sides and bottom. Clip corners, turn, and press.
- Stitch the two lining pieces together in the same way, but do not turn it right side out.

- Slip the lining inside the patchwork pocket.
- Insert the cardboard between the lining back and the pocket back. This will add stability when the pocket hangs on the wall.
- Fold the raw top edges of both the bag and lining to the inside by ½ inch (1.3 cm) and pin.

10 Make and add the strap:
- Fold the strap fabric along its length, right sides together. Stitch the long raw edges.
- Place a safety pin at one end of the strap and push it through the

strap channel to turn it right side out. Press.
- Pin the raw ends of the strap between the lining back and pocket back, 3 inches (7.6 cm) in from each side seam.

11 With a hand-sewing needle and thread, blind-stitch all around the pocket top, taking care to secure the strap with extra stitching for reinforcement.

12 Sew on bits and pieces of lace, vintage fabric trim, and doily trim to the pocket wherever you like.

Charlotte Says

- Cut up an old pillowcase or table napkin to mix into the patchwork. If these elements have stitching already on them, play off of that with similar colors or stitches.
- Allow raw edges on the front to be part of the design.
- Look through your stash for bits of quirky trim to stitch onto the patchwork, such as part of a vintage doily table runner, which can be cut apart and stitched onto the project.

Patchwork Wall Pocket Motif

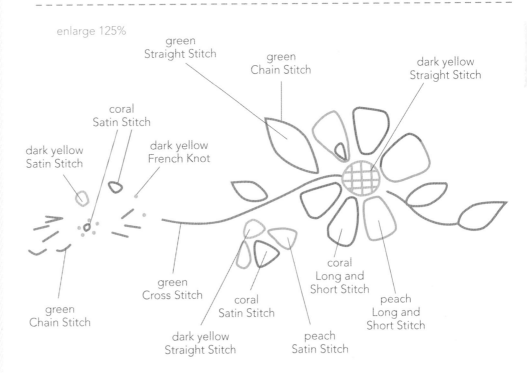

enlarge 125%

green Straight Stitch

green Chain Stitch

dark yellow Straight Stitch

coral Satin Stitch

dark yellow Satin Stitch

dark yellow French Knot

green Cross Stitch

green Chain Stitch

coral Satin Stitch

dark yellow Straight Stitch

peach Satin Stitch

coral Long and Short Stitch

peach Long and Short Stitch

Posy Pillow

A bounty of posies brings this pillow to life, with a blue coordinating cotton fabric that complements the blue embroidered flower bowl. Beautiful!

GATHER UP

Stitching Tool Kit (page 8)

Posy Pillow motif (next page)

1 piece of linen, 13 x 10 inches
(33 x 25.4 cm)

1 piece of muslin, 13 x 10 inches
(33 x 25.4 cm)

Fabric spray adhesive

Blue patterned quilting cotton,
½ yard (45.7 cm)

Blue rickrack, 1¾ yard (1.6 m), ⅜ inch
(9.5 mm) wide

Sewing machine with standard foot

Polyfill, approximately 6 ounces

Perle cotton (size 8), 1 skein each of
blue, cream, green, pale green,
light brown, light blue, blue-green,
coral, red, pale pink, dark yellow,
and hot pink

Finished dimensions: 15 x 12½ inches
(38.1 x 31.8 cm)

Seam allowance: ½ inch (1.3 mm)

STITCHES YOU'LL USE

Back stitch

Lazy daisy stitch

Satin stitch

Stem stitch

Straight stitch (also known as Running
stitch and Seed stitch)

STITCH ALONG

1 Size the motif (next page)
to measure approximately
8 x 5¼ inches (20.3 x 13.3 cm).

2 Spray the back side of
the linen with fabric spray
adhesive and place it on top
of the muslin piece.

3 Transfer the motif (see page 10)
onto the center front of the linen.

4 Secure the linen and muslin
layers in an embroidery hoop and
embroider according to the
stitch guide.

5 Take the finished piece out of the
hoop and remove any transfer
lines as needed (see page 12).
Trim the linen to measure 11 x 8½
inches (27.9 x 21.6 cm), keeping
the embroidered motif centered.

SEW ALONG

1 Cut the patterned quilting cotton
into the following pieces:
  ▸ Short sides (cut 2): 3½ x 8½
    inches (8.9 x 21.6 cm)
  ▸ Long sides (cut 2): 3½ x 16
    inches (8.9 x 40.6 cm)
  ▸ Pillow back (cut 1): 16 x 13½
    inches (40.6 x 34.3 cm)

2 Assemble the front pillow:
  ▸ With right sides together, pin
    one short side strip along
    one of the short sides of the
    embroidered linen. Stitch in
    place with a sewing machine.
    Repeat with the remaining
    short strip on the opposite
    short side of the pillow. Press.
  ▸ With right sides together,
    pin one long side strip onto
    one of the long sides of the
    front pillow and stitch with a
    sewing machine. Repeat with
    the remaining long strip on
    the remaining raw front pillow
    edge. Press all seams.

3 On the right side of the pillow back, start pinning the rickrack midway along one edge. Pin around the entire edge, aiming to keep the center of the rickrack ½ inch (1.3 cm) from the raw edge. When you reach the starting point, fold under the end of the rickrack before pinning. Machine-baste the rickrack in place.

4 Complete the pillow:

▸ With right sides together, pin the pillow front to the pillow back, aligning all four sides. Plan for a 2-inch (5.1 cm) opening on one side for turning.

▸ Machine-stitch around the perimeter.

▸ Trim the seam allowance, and clip the corners diagonally across the points.

▸ Turn the pillowcase right side out and stuff with polyfill.

▸ Sew the opening closed by hand with a whipstitch.

Charlotte Says

▸ I wanted the flower bowl to mimic blue willow pottery, but you can change the colors to white, red, or brown for a different look. Or you could just fill in the bowl shape with an interesting basket stitch.

▸ You might want to frame the piece instead of making it into a pillow.

Posy Pillow Motif

enlarge 150%

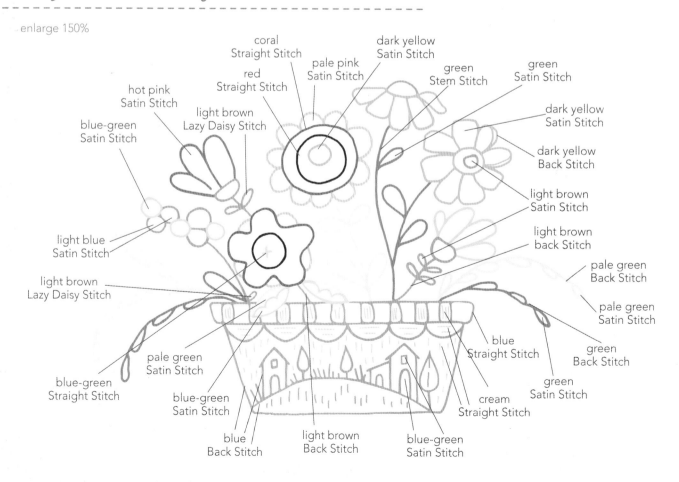

coral Straight Stitch
dark yellow Satin Stitch
red Straight Stitch
pale pink Satin Stitch
green Stem Stitch
green Satin Stitch
hot pink Satin Stitch
dark yellow Satin Stitch
light brown Lazy Daisy Stitch
blue-green Satin Stitch
dark yellow Back Stitch
light brown Satin Stitch
light blue Satin Stitch
light brown back Stitch
pale green Back Stitch
light brown Lazy Daisy Stitch
pale green Satin Stitch
blue Straight Stitch
green Back Stitch
blue-green Straight Stitch
pale green Satin Stitch
green Satin Stitch
blue-green Satin Stitch
cream Straight Stitch
blue Back Stitch
light brown Back Stitch
blue-green Satin Stitch

kitschy kitchen stitch along with *Mollie Johanson*

photo: Anna Johanson

mollie rocks

Whenever I look at Mollie's designs, I think to myself, "Yes, I can do that!" Her clean, fresh, and fun designs are exciting, not only for beginners but for experienced stitchers as well. She has a design sensibility that is minimal, playful, and downright cute. Stitch along with Mollie and discover just how much fun you can have bringing life and personality to unassuming objects, such as a toaster, mixer, cake stand, and more!

— Jenny Doh

Question: What is it about stitching that you enjoy so much?
MJ: I love that stitching is a bit like coloring. You can follow the lines or get more creative, and you can see the design coming together before your eyes. Almost from the very beginning, I started stitching my own designs based on my doodles of inanimate objects with faces. I enjoy the process of stitching so much that sometimes I even do it without an end project in mind.

Question: Do you have a special place where you like to stitch?
MJ: My favorite spot to stitch is in a chair in our living room. It's near a window where warm sunshine floods in, so it's nice and cozy with great light for seeing what I'm working on.

Question: How do you find time for embroidery?
MJ: I stitch any time I have a free moment—whether it's with my first cup of coffee in the morning, while I'm waiting for files to download on my computer, or when I'm sitting near the fireplace at night. If I'm lucky, I get a day where it's all I do!

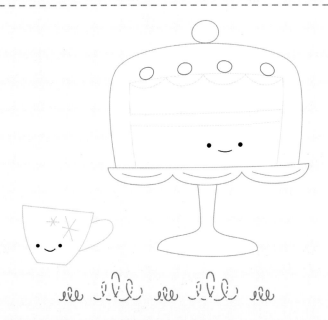

GATHER UP

Stitching Tool Kit (page 8)

Kitschy Kitchen Towel motif
(next page)

White kitchen towel

Six-strand embroidery floss, 1 skein
each of blue, taupe, and black*

Red rickrack, 19 inches (48.3 cm) long

** The designer used DMC embroidery
floss 807, 648, and 310.*

Finished dimensions: Towels shown are
18 x 28 inches (45.7 x 71.1 cm).

STITCHES YOU'LL USE

Back stitch

French knot

Running stitch (also known as
Straight stitch and Seed stitch)

Scallop stitch

Star stitch

Stem stitch

Kitschy Kitchen Towel

Start with a plain, ordinary, white kitchen towel. Then embroider a place setting motif and add a length of bright red rickrack to make it kitschy-extraordinary!

STITCH ALONG

1 Wash and dry the towel.

2 The motif (next page) is shown actual size; approximately 4 x 3 inches (10.2 x 7.6 cm). Enlarge or reduce the motif size as desired.

3 Trace the motif onto tracing paper, then pin the paper to the center bottom edge of the towel.

Transfer Hints

The towel used for this project had a bit of texture, making it difficult to trace the motif onto the fabric. So Mollie traced it onto tracing paper, then pinned the paper in place in the center at the bottom edge of the towel. If your towel also has texture, follow the steps outlined in the instructions. If your towel does not have as much texture, use one of the standard transferring methods (see page 10), secure the towel in an embroidery hoop, and embroider according to the stitch guide.

4 Stitching through the tracing paper and the towel without an embroidery hoop, embroider according to the stitch guide. To ensure that the stitching does not come undone in the wash, secure the ends with small, strong knots.

5 Carefully tear away the tracing paper, making sure none of the embroidery is disturbed.

6 Pin the rickrack along the bottom edge of the towel, folding under both ends. Use red embroidery floss to stitch the rickrack with a running stitch, removing the pins as you go.

Kitschy Kitchen Towel Motif

shown actual size

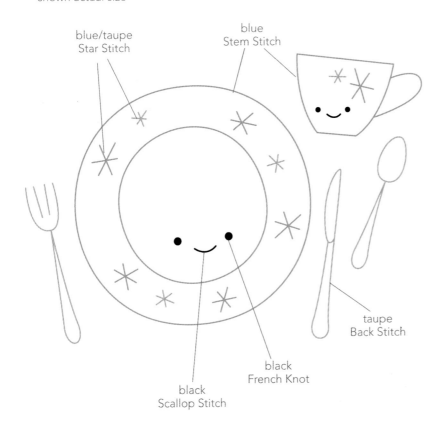

blue/taupe
Star Stitch

blue
Stem Stitch

taupe
Back Stitch

black
French Knot

black
Scallop Stitch

Mollie Says

► For the eyes and mouth on the teacup, I used two strands of floss. On everything else, I used three strands of floss.

► For embroidered items that will be washed, it is a good idea to wash and dry the item before stitching.

► Choose a detail element from the pattern you're using (such as the stars) and stitch it in the corner where you might hang the towel. It adds a little something extra special!

Freshly Baked Curtain

Who knew that curtains could have so much personality? Transfer these cheerful designs onto plain premade curtains to make your kitchen as cute as can be.

GATHER UP

Stitching Tool Kit (page 8)

Freshly Baked motifs (next page)

White cotton café-style curtain
to fit your window

Six-strand embroidery floss,
1 skein each of black, taupe,
yellow, red, and blue*

** The designer used DMC
embroidery floss 310, 648,
734, 606, and 807.*

Finished dimensions: Curtains
shown are 56 x 30 inches
(142.2 x 76.2 cm).

STITCHES YOU'LL USE

Back stitch

French knot

Scallop stitch

Stem stitch

STITCH ALONG

1 Size the motifs (next page)
as follows:

  ▸ Electric mixer: approximately
    4 x 4¼ inches (10.2 x 10.9 cm)

  ▸ Recipe box: approximately
    3½ x 4 inches (8.9 x 10.2 cm)

  ▸ Cake stand: approximately
    3½ x 4 inches (8.9 x 10.2 cm)

2 Transfer the recipe box motif
(see page 10) onto the center
right edge of the curtain panel.
Transfer the electric mixer motif
to the top right edge and the
cake plate motif to the bottom
right edge of the panel. Transfer
just the star motif from the center
of the recipe box motif two
times—first centered in between
the mixer and recipe box, and then
centered in between the recipe
box and cake stand, making sure
to rotate the star by 90°.

3 Secure the recipe box motif in an
embroidery hoop and embroider
according to the stitch guide.
Remove any transfer lines as
needed (see page 12). Repeat
with the other two motifs.

Freshly Baked Curtain Motifs

enlarge 125%

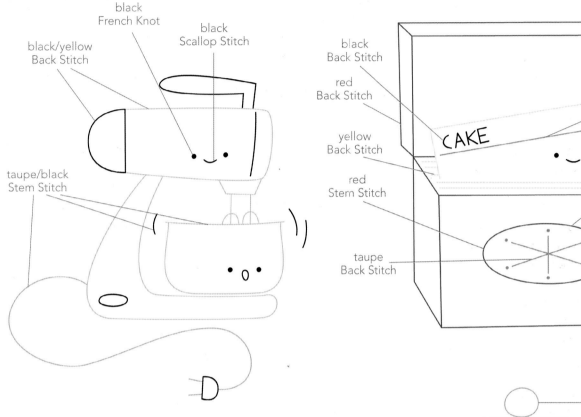

black/yellow
Back Stitch

black
French Knot

black
Scallop Stitch

taupe/black
Stem Stitch

black
Back Stitch

red
Back Stitch

yellow
Back Stitch

red
Stem Stitch

taupe
Back Stitch

taupe
Stem Stitch

taupe
French Knot

CAKE

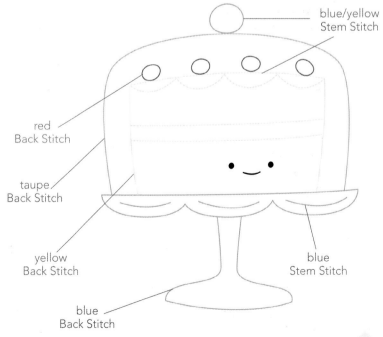

blue/yellow
Stem Stitch

red
Back Stitch

taupe
Back Stitch

yellow
Back Stitch

blue
Back Stitch

blue
Stem Stitch

Mollie Says

▸ For the red recipe box, the yellow
and black parts of the mixer, and the
blue base and taupe glass dome of
the cake stand, I used six strands
of floss. On everything else, I used
three strands of floss.

▸ You can add extra detail to your
curtain with running stitches along
the edges or on the tabs at the top.
Running stitches make things cute!

Retro Hot Pad

The groovy embroidery makes this hot pad adorable on the outside, and the insulated batting makes it practical on the inside. Roll a set of wooden serving spoons with one, tie it with ribbon, and serve it up as a hostess gift!

GATHER UP

Stitching Tool Kit (page 8)
Retro Hot Pad motif (next page)
White cotton fabric, 9-inch
　(22.9 cm) square
Six-strand embroidery floss, 1 skein
　each of taupe, light brown, and
　black*
Burnt orange cotton fabric:
　1 piece 9 inch (22.9 cm) square;
　1 piece 2 x 8 inches (5.2 x 20.3 cm)
Thin cotton batting:
　9-inch (22.9 cm) square
Insulated batting:
　9-inch (22.9 cm) square
Sewing machine with standard foot
Iron and ironing board

*The designer used DMC embroidery
　floss 648, 435, and 310*

Finished dimensions: 8 inches
(20.3 cm) square

Seam allowance: ½ inch (1.3 cm)

STITCHES YOU'LL USE

Back stitch
Couching stitch
French knot
Scallop stitch
Stem stitch

STITCH AND SEW ALONG

1 Size the motif to approximately 4½ x 4 inches (11.4 x 10.2 cm).

2 Transfer the toaster motif (see page 10) onto the right side of the white cotton fabric. Place it onto an embroidery hoop and embroider according to the stitch guide. Remove any transfer lines as needed (see page 12).

3 To prepare the hanging loop, fold and press the orange fabric strip as you would if making double-fold bias tape (press in half along its length, open it up, press the long edges into the center, then repress in half). Sew the long open edge with a running stitch and light brown embroidery floss.

4 Lay the thin cotton batting onto your work surface. Place the insulated batting onto the thin cotton batting, followed by the embroidered piece facing up, and the burnt orange fabric right side down. Fold the loop from step 3 in half and tuck it between the embroidered piece and the burnt orange fabric, with the raw ends positioned at the top left corner. Pin the layers together.

5 Use a sewing machine to stitch along all edges, leaving a 2-inch (5.1 cm) gap along the bottom edge.

6 Clip the corners of the fabric, and cut away some of the batting along the edges to reduce bulk. Turn the hot pad right side out and whip stitch the gap closed.

7 Add a running stitch border along the edges with three strands of light brown embroidery floss.

Mollie Says

▶ I used six strands of floss on the body of the toaster and the swirl design on the toaster. For everything else, I used three strands of floss.

▶ Since hot pads are likely to go through the wash, it's a good idea to use knots to secure your thread so that your stitching doesn't come undone.

Retro Hot Pad Motif

enlarge 125%

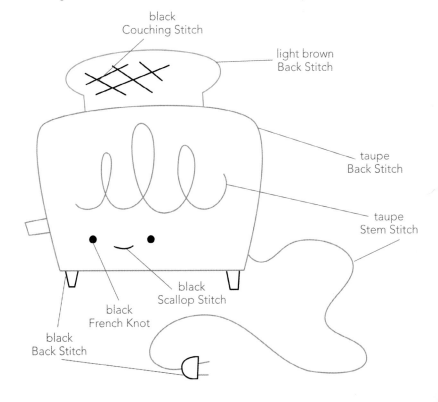

black
Couching Stitch

light brown
Back Stitch

taupe
Back Stitch

taupe
Stem Stitch

black
Scallop Stitch

black
French Knot

black
Back Stitch

camping chic stitch along with *Liesi Cross*

photo: Bryan Smith

liesi creates quirky designs

Liesi's great use of letters and shapes first attracted me to her work, and I haven't looked back since. I think it takes a special talent to be able to stitch letters in the cute, fun way that Liesi does, and she even takes her letters a step further by complementing them with charming, simple shapes created in a great assortment of stitches. Stitch along with Liesi and learn how to share your favorite messages and quirky shapes with assorted fabrics and fibers!

— Jenny Doh

Question: Why do you like the art of stitching?

LC: Stitching gives me time to think and a chance to find solitude within a busy day. I started embroidering in my early twenties, and now I can't put the needle down for the life of me. I crave the peace that embroidery offers.

Question: Are there times when you avoid stitching?

LC: I try not to stitch when I'm in a hurry. This defeats the purpose I'm looking for, plus I'm bound to make mistakes. If I'm feeling flustered or rushed as I stitch, all I need to do is step away for a few minutes and take a breather. Then I can come back to my work refreshed and ready to go.

Question: Do you prefer simple designs or more complex ones?

LC: This is actually one reason stitching is so appealing to me—its versatility. You can make something intricate, such as a full-blown portrait, or something simple. Either way the finished piece, with all the different stitches and colors, is bound to be interesting to see and magical to run your hands across.

Mountain Eye Mask

For those who don't want to wake up with the sun during camping trips, this eye mask will help keep the light out. Sleep in for as long as you wish!

STITCH AND SEW ALONG

1 The motif (next page) is shown actual size; approximately 5½ x 2½ inches (14 x 6.4 cm). Enlarge or reduce the motif as desired.

2 Transfer the eye mask template to the right side of the black fabric. Transfer the motif (see page 10) to the center front of the marked mask area.

3 Secure the fabric in an embroidery hoop and embroider according to the stitch guide. Remove the finished piece from the hoop and cut the fabric along the template lines. Remove any transfer lines as needed (see page 12).

4 Pin the mask template to the felt and cut it out. With wrong sides together, pin the embroidered piece to the felt piece.

5 Insert one end of the elastic in between the layers of fabric and felt on one side and pin. Place the mask on your eyes and wrap the elastic around your head to find where you need to trim the elastic to fit your head. Trim as needed and insert the opposite end of the elastic in between the layers of fabric and felt on the opposite side of the mask and pin.

6 Use a sewing machine to stitch along the entire outer edge of the mask, making sure to catch both ends of the elastic.

7 Add straight stitch embroidery along the sewn edge with perle cotton.

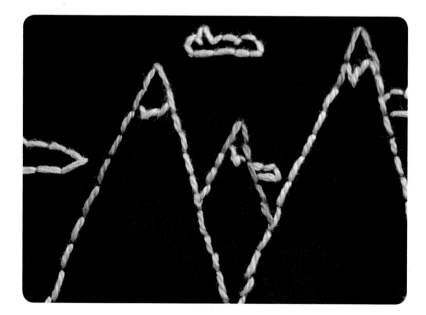

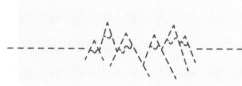

GATHER UP

Stitching Tool Kit (page 8)
Mountain Eye Mask motif (next page)
Eye Mask template (next page)
1 piece of black cotton fabric: 8½ x 5 inches (21.6 x 12.7 cm)
Six-strand embroidery floss, 1 skein of light blue
Perle cotton, 1 skein (size 5) of variegated brown/beige
1 sheet of black craft felt: 8½ x 10 inches (21.6 x 25.4 cm)
Elastic: measured and cut to fit the size of your head
Sewing machine with standard foot

Finished dimensions: 7 x 3 inches (17.8 x 7.6 cm)

STITCHES YOU'LL USE

Back stitch
Straight stitch (also known as Running stitch and Seed stitch)

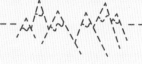

Mountain Eye Mask Motif & Template

shown actual size

light blue
Back Stitch

variegated
Back Stitch
(Perle cotton)

Liesl Says

▶ I used six strands of floss
for all of the clouds. For
everything else, I used
perle cotton.

Eye Mask Template

GATHER UP

Stitching Tool Kit (page 8)

Let's Camp Drawstring Bag motif
(next page)

2 pieces of solid green cotton fabric,
10 x 10½ inches (25.4 x 26.7 cm) each

Yellow and green worsted-weight acrylic
yarn, less than 1 skein of each

Yarn needle

Six-strand embroidery floss, 1 skein
each of brown, rust, light blue, pink,
orange, purple, red, green, white,
light pink, mint, dark green, yellow,
and dark brown

Perle cotton (size 5), 1 skein of
variegated green/brown/beige

Sewing machine with standard foot

Finished dimensions: 9 x 9½ inches
(22.9 x 24.1 cm)

Seam allowances: ⅛ inch (3 mm) and
¼ inch (6 mm)

STITCHES YOU'LL USE

Back stitch
Chain stitch
French knot
Satin stitch
Straight stitch

Let's Camp Drawstring Bag

Whip up this easy peasy bag to hold all of your camping essentials. Heck, since they're so fun to make, why not create one for everyone you invite to your next outing?

STITCH AND SEW ALONG

1 Size the motif (next page) to approximately 7 x 8 inches (17.8 x 20 cm).

2 Transfer the motif (see page 10) to the center front of one piece of green cotton fabric.

3 Secure the fabric with the motif in an embroidery hoop and embroider according to the stitch guide. When you embroider the letter C and the top portion of the letter T with the yarn, use the yarn needle to make the stitches.

4 Take the finished piece out of the hoop and remove any transfer lines as needed (see page 12).

5 With wrong sides facing, pin the two green fabrics together and stitch along the bottom edge with a ⅛-inch (3 mm) seam allowance.

6 On the front and back sides of the bag, cut notches 1½ inches (3.8 cm) from the top edge on both the left and right sides.

7 Sew one of the sides starting from the sewn bottom edge with a ⅛-inch (3 mm) seam allowance, stopping at the notch. Repeat this step for the other side.

8 Flip the bag wrong side out and sew the bottom edge with a ¼-inch (6 mm) seam allowance. Sew one of the sides with a ¼-inch (6 mm) seam allowance, starting from the bottom seam, stopping at the notch. Repeat this step for the other side. You have just created French seams with all raw edges enclosed.

9 With the wrong side of the embroidered fabric facing you, fold and press the raw (vertical) unsewn 1½-inch (3.8 cm) sections in by ¼ inch (6 mm) on both the left and right sides. Sew these sections in place, making sure to backstitch at the start and end points. Fold and press the top raw edge down by ¼ inch (6 mm) and sew across.

10 Fold the top edge down again, so that the fold is at the side notch marks, and sew in place, making sure to backstitch at the start and end points. You have now completed the drawstring channel for the front side.

11 Repeat steps 9 and 10 for the back side of the bag.

12 Use a yarn needle to thread an approximately 24-inch (64.4 cm) piece of yarn through the front and back drawstring channels.

13 Turn the bag right side out.

Let's Camp Drawstring Bag Motif

enlarge 150%

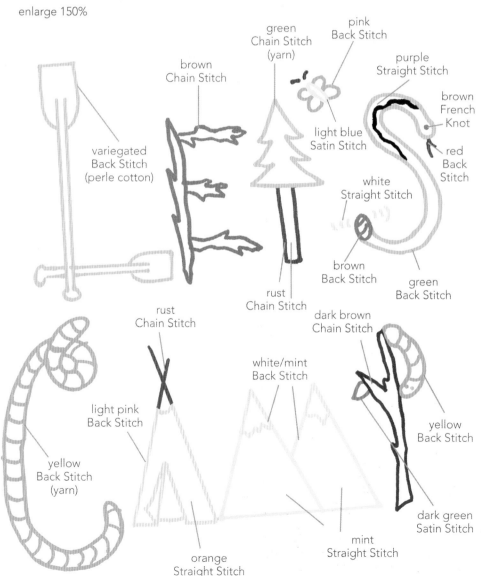

variegated Back Stitch (perle cotton)

brown Chain Stitch

green Chain Stitch (yarn)

pink Back Stitch

purple Straight Stitch

brown French Knot

red Back Stitch

light blue Satin Stitch

white Straight Stitch

brown Back Stitch

green Back Stitch

rust Chain Stitch

rust Chain Stitch

dark brown Chain Stitch

white/mint Back Stitch

yellow Back Stitch (yarn)

light pink Back Stitch

yellow Back Stitch

orange Straight Stitch

mint Straight Stitch

dark green Satin Stitch

Liesi Says

▸ For the "teepee" A, fill-stitch by starting with a bottom row of long verticle straight stitches using six strands of floss. on the next row above, use five strands. On the next row above, use three strands. On the top row, use one strand.

▸ I used six strands of floss for everything else except for the letters L, C, and the "tree" portion of the letter T, as noted.

Mini Camping Pillow

This cozy pillow can serve as both tent décor and a comfy nighttime head support—a must for your next crafty camping excursion.

STITCH AND SEW ALONG

1 The motif (next page) is shown actual size; approximately 8 x 6 inches (20 x 15.2 cm). Enlarge or reduce the motif as desired.

2 Transfer the motif (see page 10) to the center of the linen.

3 Secure the fabric with the motif in an embroidery hoop and embroider according to the stitch guide. When you embroider the tree portions with the yarn, use the yarn needle to make the stitches.

Take the finished piece out of the hoop and remove any transfer lines as needed (see page 12).

4 Pin the embroidered linen and patterned cotton together with right sides facing. Plan for a 1½-inch (3.8 cm) centered opening on one of the long sides by double-pinning on both sides of the opening. Start stitching at one of the double pins and stitch around all sides, backstitching at the start and end points.

GATHER UP

Stitching Tool Kit (page 8)
Mini Camping Pillow motif
   (next page)
1 piece of gray medium-weight
   linen: 10 x 9 inches
   (25.4 x 22.9 cm)
Dark green and yellow worsted-
   weight acrylic yarns, less than
   1 skein of each
Yarn needle
Six-strand embroidery floss,
   1 skein each of rust, gold,
   and brown
1 piece of brown patterned
   cotton, 10 x 9 inches
   (25.4 x 22.9 cm)
Sewing machine with
   standard foot
Polyester fiberfill, 20-ounce bag

Finished dimensions: 9 x 7 inches
(22.9 x 17.8 cm)

Seam allowance: ½ inch (1.3 cm)

STITCHES YOU'LL USE

Back stitch
Long and short stitch
Star stitch
Straight stitch (also known as
   Running stitch and Seed stitch)

5 Trim the seam and cut corners at a diagonal. Turn the pillowcase right side out through the opening.

6 Stuff the pillowcase with polyester fiberfill until you reach a firmness that you like.

7 Topstitch the opening closed with the seam allowance tucked into the seam.

Liesi Says

▸ I used three strands of floss for the brown horizon line and six strands of floss for everything else except for the green and yellow yarn for the trees, as noted.

Mini Camping Pillow Motif

shown actual size

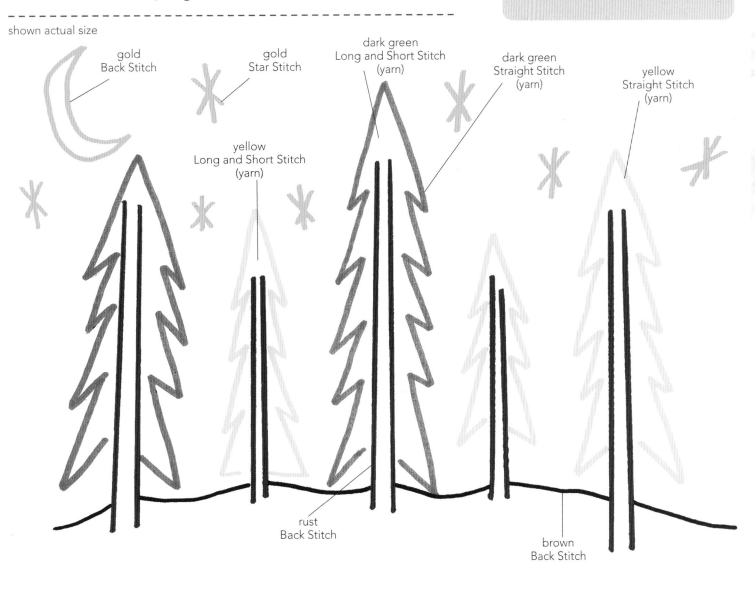

unusual creatures stitch along
with *Megan Eckman*

photo: Jeffrey Opp

megan masterfully illustrates

Megan's skillset as both an illustrator and a stitcher first drew me to her work. She has a special talent for producing amazing pen-and-ink illustrations and then transferring those illustrations into embroidery patterns. When I look at her work, I can almost picture her pen sketching on a piece of paper, because her projects use such artful mark-making. Stitch along with Megan to discover how to illustrate simply with a needle and thread.

— Jenny Doh

Question: Why is stitching special to you?
ME: Stitching always brings up memories of learning to sew days-of-the-week kittens with my grandmother on rainy days at the lake. I loved these sentimental patterns as a young girl, but I'm glad that iron-on transfers have expanded into a wider variety of patterns and illustrations. I think the evolution of patterns has made stitching more appealing to a larger group of people.

Question: How does stitching fit in with your love of illustration?
ME: Stitching has allowed me to turn my pen-and-ink illustrations into a new medium that other people can make for themselves. I'm always experimenting with transforming my drawings into easy-to-follow patterns. I usually stitch late at night while watching a movie; I prefer not to stitch first thing in the morning because my fingers need to loosen up.

Question: What are your goals as an embroidery artist?
ME: My goal as an artist is to help people rekindle their wonder and imagination. I hope that seeing my pen-and-ink illustrations in stitched form will open peoples' minds about what they can do with a simple needle and thread.

African Wild Dog

African Wild Dog Pillow

This artful pillow features the mighty African Wild Dog, made with a series of split embroidery stitches. The pillow would fit well on the bed or chair of an animal lover.

STITCH ALONG

1 The motif (next page) is shown actual size; approximately 7 x 8 inches (17.8 x 20.3 cm). Enlarge or reduce the motif size as desired.

2 Transfer the motif (see page 10) onto the right side of the cotton canvas piece. Secure the fabric in an embroidery hoop and embroider according to the stitch guide.

3 Take the finished piece out of the hoop and remove any transfer lines as needed (see page 12).

4 Make an envelope back for the pillow:
   ▸ Take a black fabric piece and make a ¼-inch (6 mm) double-fold hem on one of the long sides. Repeat with the remaining black fabric.
   ▸ Lay the embroidered fabric onto your table face up. Place the larger backing piece face down, aligning the long raw edge with the top edge of the embroidered piece.
   ▸ Place the smaller backing piece face down on top of the larger backing piece, aligning the long raw edge with the bottom of the embroidered piece. Pin all three pieces of fabric together.
   ▸ Stitch all four sides of the pinned layers.

5 Cut all trailing threads, and trim excess fabric along the edges and corners. Flip the pillowcase right side out and insert a 12-inch (30.5 cm) square pillow form.

GATHER UP

Stitching Tool Kit (page 8)
African Wild Dog motif (next page)
1 piece of cotton-blend canvas fabric: 13 inches (33 cm) square
Six-strand embroidery floss, 1 skein each of black, blue, and yellow*
Sewing machine with standard foot
2 pieces of black cotton-blend backing fabric:
▸ 13 x 9½ inches (33 x 24.1 cm)
▸ 13 x 6½ inches (33 x 16.5 cm)
Pillow form, 12 inches (30.5 cm) square

* The designer used DMC embroidery floss 310, 995, and 307

Finished dimensions: 12 inches (30.5 cm) square

Seam allowance: ½ inch (1.3 cm)

STITCHES YOU'LL USE

Split stitch
Straight stitch (also known as Running stitch and Seed stitch)

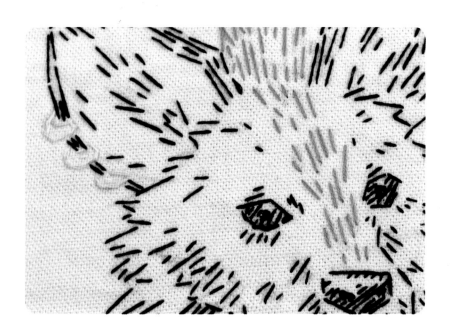

African Wild Dog Pillow Motif

shown actual size

yellow
Split Stitch

black
Straight Stitch

black
Split Stitch

blue
Straight Stitch

Megan Says

▶ I used two strands of floss for all the embroidery.
▶ For the backing fabric, you can use a contrasting black fabric like I did, or you can use the same color as the front of the pillow.

African Wild Dog

Pyjama Squid Hoop Art

It's just one of those pyjama-wearing days for this squid who's in the mood to relax and just lounge around the house. A split stitch is all that Megan used to make the squid and its pink pyjamas come to life.

GATHER UP

Stitching Tool Kit (page 8)
Pyjama Squid motif (next page)
8-inch (20.3 cm) wooden
   embroidery hoop
Black spray paint
1 piece of cotton canvas, 10 inches
   (25.4 cm) square
Six-strand embroidery floss, 1 skein
   each of black and pink*
Mod Podge
26 inches (66 cm) of black ribbon,
   ¼ inch (6 mm) wide

*The designer used DMC embroidery
   floss 310, and 760*

Finished dimensions: the hoop is
8 inches (20.3 cm) in diameter

STITCHES
YOU'LL USE

Split stitch

STITCH ALONG

1 Spray paint the outer portion of the hoop with black spray paint and let it dry.

2 Size the motif (below) to approximately 6 inches (15.2 cm) wide.

3 Transfer the motif (see page 10) onto the right side of the cotton canvas. Secure the fabric in an embroidery hoop and embroider according to the stitch guide.

4 Take the finished piece out of the hoop and remove any transfer lines as needed (see page 12). When the fabric is dry, secure it back onto the embroidery hoop and center the motif with the metal closure at the top.

5 Cut the edges of the fabric, leaving just enough to wrap around the inside back of the hoop. Fold over and glue this excess fabric to the inner hoop using Mod Podge. Let it dry.

6 Glue the ribbon over the glued canvas on the inside of the inner hoop using Mod Podge. Let dry.

Megan Says

▶ I used two strands of floss and the split stitch for the entire piece.

Pyjama Squid Hoop Art Motif

shown actual size

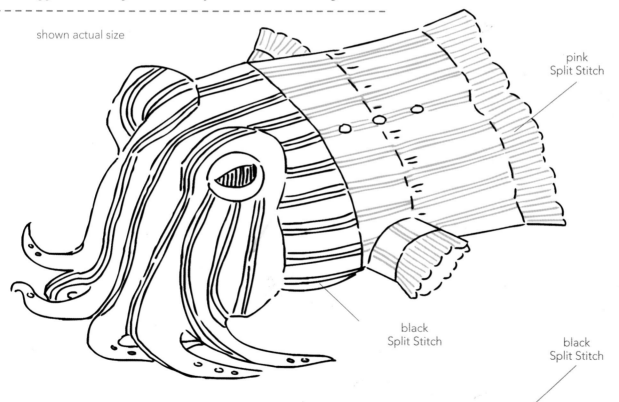

pink Split Stitch

black Split Stitch

black Split Stitch

Pyjama Squid

GATHER UP

Stitching Tool Kit (page 8)

Bearded Clams Pouch motif (next page)

Cotton canvas, two 9 x 12-inch
(22.9 x 30.5 cm) pieces

Embroidery floss, 1 skein each of black,
gray, pale yellow, orange, and brown*

Sewing machine with standard foot

32 inches (81.3 cm) of tan ribbon, ½ inch
(1.3 cm) wide

** The designer used DMC embroidery
floss 310, 646, 745, 742, and 434*

Finished dimensions: 8 x 10½ inches
(20.3 x 26.7 cm)

Seam allowance: ½ inch (1.3 cm)

STITCHES YOU'LL USE

Split stitch

Straight stitch (also known as Running
stitch and Seed stitch)

Bearded Clams Pouch

Anyone who likes a subdued yet playful design will enjoy filling this sturdy pouch with all sorts of things.

STITCH AND SEW ALONG

1 Size the motif (next page) to approximately 7¼ x 7¾ inches (18.4 x 19.7 cm).

2 Transfer the motif (see page 10) onto the right side of one of the cotton canvas pieces. Secure the fabric in an embroidery hoop and embroider according to the stitch guide.

3 Take the fabric out of the hoop and remove any transfer lines as needed (see page 12).

4 Stitch the pouch front and back:
- ▶ Lay the embroidered piece on your work surface, facing up. Pin the second piece of cotton canvas on top with right side facing down, and all edges aligned.
- ▶ Measure 2 inches (5.2 cm) down from the top edge and make a mark on the left and right sides.
- ▶ Stitch down the left side starting at the 2-inch (5.1 cm) mark, across the bottom, and up the right side to the 2-inch (5.1 cm) mark.

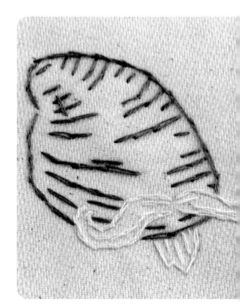

5 Make the casing:
- ▶ Fold all four side raw edges of the top unsewn 2 inches (5.1 cm) to the wrong side by the same width as the seam allowance and pin. Stitch near the raw edge of one of the folded sections to tack

it down. Repeat with the other three raw folded sections.
- ▶ Make a ½-inch (1.3 cm) double-fold hem on both the front and back of the bag. Trim trailing threads and flip the bag right side out.

6 Attach a safety pin to one end of the ribbon. Feed the ribbon through the casing on one side and then the other. Knot the ends of the ribbon to keep them from slipping out of the casing.

Bearded Clams Pouch Motif

enlarge 150%

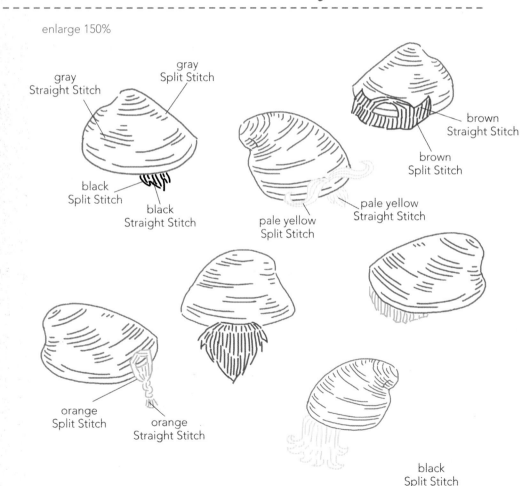

gray
Straight Stitch

gray
Split Stitch

brown
Straight Stitch

brown
Split Stitch

black
Split Stitch

black
Straight Stitch

pale yellow
Split Stitch

pale yellow
Straight Stitch

orange
Split Stitch

orange
Straight Stitch

black
Split Stitch

Bearded Clams

Megan Says

- ▶ I used two strands of floss on all the embroidery.
- ▶ For the gray clams, I used a split stitch to outline the shells and embroider the curved lines in the shells. For the straight and short lines in the shells, I used straight stitches.
- ▶ For the beards, I used a split stitch for all curved lines and straight stitches for all the straight, short lines.
- ▶ You can use any color ribbon for the bag closure.

all about robots stitch along
with *Carina Envoldsen-Harris*

photo by artist

carina creates joy

Carina's designs just exude joy and fun. I love that whether she is stitching a traditional-looking pattern or something more light-hearted, she always uses bright color combinations that bring a modern feel to her work. At first glance, Carina's designs appear intricate and detailed, but upon closer examination her designs combine beautiful and simple shapes and curves in an original way, making her patterns achievable for stitchers of all levels. Stitch along with Carina to make your own color-filled works of joy!

— Jenny Doh

Question: Why does the art of stitching appeal to you?
CEH: Embroidery is a beautifully tactile way of creating color. It's as if I'm painting with a needle and thread instead of a paintbrush, but the thread adds a dimensional texture that is just wonderful to run your hands across. I've been painting and drawing in addition to embroidering for as long as I can remember, so the colorful aspect of stitching really appeals to me.

Question: Where do you usually stitch?
CEH: I usually work on my embroidery sitting on the sofa while I'm listening to music and podcasts or watching documentaries on television. But the great thing about stitching is that it can be done anywhere—I've even stitched on a train 250 feet (75 meters) under the English Channel!

Question: What is your favorite thing about embroidery?
CEH: Stitching relaxes me, and it's so doable. Not only are embroidery materials transportable, but they are also affordable, and embroidery can be used in so many ways—from embellishing clothing to making home décor. But perhaps my favorite thing about embroidery is that the basics are fairly easy to learn, yet there is so much to the art. I'm always learning new stitches and exploring their possibilities.

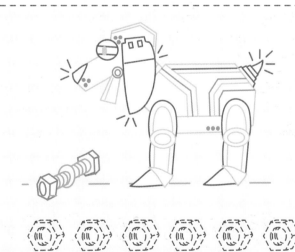

Robot Dog Tote

A pre-made tote bag makes this a speedy project to create. Pack it full of Fido's toys, make it your go-to library bag, or give it as a gift to a lucky friend.

GATHER UP

Stitching Tool Kit (page 8)
Robot Dog Tote motif (next page)
1 lightweight canvas tote bag
    (see tote specs)
Six-strand embroidery floss, 1 skein
    each of orange, red, apple green,
    grass green, light blue, blue, light
    turquoise, and turquoise*

*The designer used DMC embroidery
    floss 606, 321, 703, 701, 996, 995,
    3846, and 3843*

Finished dimensions: Tote shown is
14 x 16 inches (35.6 x 40.6 cm)

Tote specs: Blank canvas tote bags are available in assorted sizes at craft stores. Lightweight canvas bags are easier to work with in an embroidery hoop. Be sure to get one large enough so that the area that you are embroidering can fit comfortably onto the hoop.

STITCHES YOU'LL USE

Back stitch
French knot
Satin stitch
Straight stitch (also known as Running
    stitch and Seed stitch)

STITCH ALONG

1 The motif (below) is shown actual size; approximately 6 x 4 inches (15.2 x 10.2 cm). Enlarge or reduce the motif as desired.

2 Transfer the motif (see page 10) to the tote bag, positioned toward the upper right corner.

3 Secure the section of the tote with the transferred motif onto an embroidery hoop and embroider according to the stitch guide.

4 Remove the tote from the hoop and remove any transfer lines as needed (see page 12). Press the tote with an iron if needed.

Carina Says

▶ I used three strands of floss on all the stitches.

Robot Dog Tote Motif

shown actual size

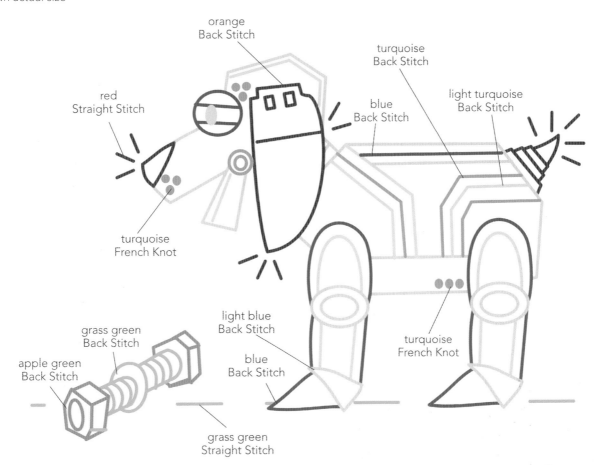

orange
Back Stitch

turquoise
Back Stitch

red
Straight Stitch

light turquoise
Back Stitch

blue
Back Stitch

turquoise
French Knot

grass green
Back Stitch

apple green
Back Stitch

light blue
Back Stitch

blue
Back Stitch

turquoise
French Knot

grass green
Straight Stitch

Robot Boy Portrait

Embroidery placed in a hoop becomes wall art that's ready to hang in no time flat. Consider doing a whole family of robot portraits with hoops in various sizes.

GATHER UP

Stitching Tool Kit (page 8)
Robot Boy Portrait motif (page 66)
Piece of white cotton fabric, 10 inches (25.4 cm) square
Wooden embroidery hoop, 6 inches (15.2 cm) in diameter
Six-strand embroidery floss, 1 skein each of yellow, orange, red, dark turquoise, sky blue, lilac, dark lilac, mint, light mint, and light green.*
Turquoise rickrack, 19 inches (48.3 cm) long
White craft felt at least 6 inches (15.2 cm) square

The designer used DMC embroidery floss 307, 947, 606, 666, 3845, 996, 155, 552, 954, 912, and 734

Finished dimensions: 6 inches (15.2 cm) in diameter

STITCH AND SEW ALONG

1 Size the Robot Boy motif (page 66) to approximately 4½ inches (11.4 cm) in diameter.

2 Transfer the motif (see page 10) to the center of the white cotton fabric piece.

3 Secure the fabric in the embroidery hoop and embroider according to the stitch guide. Take the finished piece out of the hoop and remove any transfer lines as needed (see page 12).

4 Insert the fabric and rickrack into the hoop as follows:
▸ Place the embroidered fabric on top of the inner ring of the hoop.

STITCHES YOU'LL USE

Back stitch
Straight stitch (also known as Running stitch and Seed stitch)
Satin stitch

▸ Loosen the outer hoop ring as much as possible without taking out the screw completely. Place the outer ring around the fabric and inner ring, making sure that the screw is at the top.

▸ Insert the rickrack between the fabric and the outer ring, allowing for a slight overlap with the ends. With a bit of patience, this tricky step can be done!

5 Cut the white craft felt into a circle 6 inches (15.2 cm) in diameter. Check to see if it fits easily within the inner ring of the embroidery hoop and trim the circle as needed. Spray fabric spray adhesive to one side of the felt circle and place it inside the inner ring on the back side of the work.

6 Trim the fabric into a circular shape, leaving 2 inches (5.1 cm) all around the hoop. At the edge of the fabric, make a row of running straight stitches then pull the fabric tight toward the center as if you were making a fabric yo-yo. Tie off the sewing thread.

7 Thread a piece of rickrack through the screw at the top of the hoop and tie the ends together to make a loop. Use the loop to hang on a wall.

Robot Boy Portrait Motif

enlarge 125%

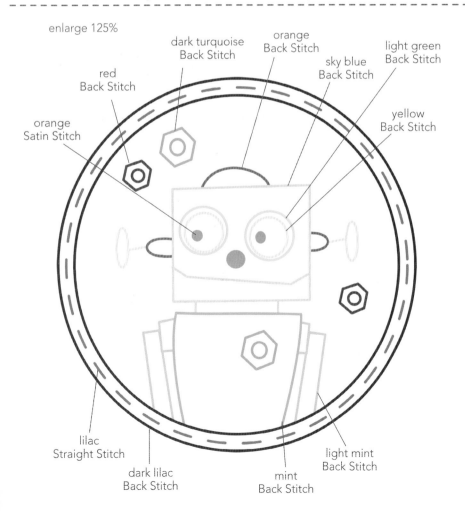

red
Back Stitch

dark turquoise
Back Stitch

orange
Back Stitch

sky blue
Back Stitch

light green
Back Stitch

orange
Satin Stitch

yellow
Back Stitch

lilac
Straight Stitch

dark lilac
Back Stitch

mint
Back Stitch

light mint
Back Stitch

Carina Says

▸ I used three strands of embroidery floss on all stitches.

▸ Consider spray-painting the embroidery hoop with a color that coordinates with the décor before attaching the embroidery to it.

Robot Heads Cuff

What's more hip than a cuff with three embroidered robot heads? Embroidered robot heads with a touch of neon-colored floss, of course!

STITCH ALONG

1 The motif (next page) is shown actual size; approximately 4½ x 1⅛ inches (11.4 x 2.8 cm). Enlarge or reduce the motif as desired.

2 Transfer the cuff template (see page 10) to the right side of the linen, horizontally. Transfer the motif to the center of the marked cuff area.

3 Secure the linen onto an embroidery hoop and embroider according to the stitch guide.

4 Cut the linen along the cuff template lines. Remove any transfer lines as needed (see page 12).

5 Following manufacturer's instructions, press the interfacing to the back side of the linen piece with an iron.

6 Place the lining fabric on top of the embroidered linen, with right sides facing each other, and pin together.

7 Fold the leather cord in half to make a loop and insert the loop end between the two fabric layers at one short edge. Let the ends of the leather cord stick out ¼ inch (6 mm) beyond the fabric edge, and pin in place.

8 Mark a 3-inch (7.6 cm) turning gap along one long edge with double pins.

GATHER UP

Stitching Tool Kit (page 8)
Robot Heads motif (next page)
Cuff template (next page)
Lightweight linen fabric, 9 x 7 inches (22.9 x 17.8 cm) for front
Six-strand embroidery floss, 1 skein each of orange, dark salmon, magenta, and neon yellow*
Lime green quilting cotton, 7½ x 2½ inches (19 x 6.4 cm) for lining
Iron-on lightweight interfacing: 7½ x 2½ inches (19 x 6.4 cm)
1/16-inch-wide (1.6 mm) leather cord, 3½ inches (8.9 cm) long
Sewing machine with standard foot
Turning tool, such as a chopstick or pencil with an eraser tip
1 lime green button, ⅝ inch (1.6 cm) in diameter

The designer used DMC embroidery floss 608, 891, 917, and 980

Finished dimensions: 7 x 2 inches (17.8 x 5.1 cm)

Seam allowance: ¼ inch (6 mm)

STITCHES YOU'LL USE

Back stitch
French knot

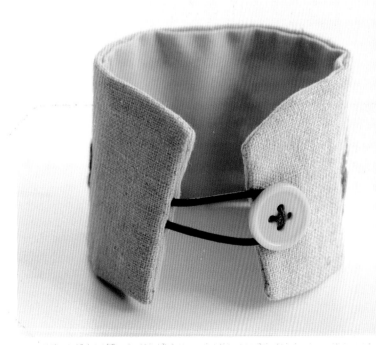

9 Use a sewing machine to sew the layers together, starting at one double pin point and ending at the other double pin point.

10 Clip the corners, and trim off a bit of the seam allowance and excess leather cord to reduce bulk.

11 Turn the cuff right side out through the turning gap and use a turning tool to push out the corners so that they are crisp and pointy.

12 With a hand-sewing needle and thread, use a slip stitch to sew the turning gap closed.

13 Hand-sew the button on the opposite side from the leather cord.

Carina Says

▸ I used three strands of floss on all the stitches.

▸ You can use elastic instead of leather cord, which will make the size of the cuff more flexible.

Robot Heads Cuff Motif & Template

shown actual size

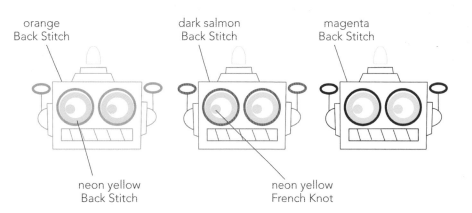

orange
Back Stitch

dark salmon
Back Stitch

magenta
Back Stitch

neon yellow
Back Stitch

neon yellow
French Knot

Cuff Template

sewing notions stitch along with *Sami Teasdale*

photo by artist

sami's stitches are cute as buttons

Sami's designs are lovely and engaging. Her love of nature—especially birds—shines through beautifully in her work. I'm particularly fond of her buttons, such small treasures that speak volumes in the details. I could easily add any of her stitched buttons to my favorite trench coat, jacket, or sweater. Stitch along with Sami to learn her clean, precise style, and find inspiration in her elegant simplicity.

— Jenny Doh

Question: What first drew you to the art of stitching?
ST: I was lucky to grow up recognizing and appreciating the beauty of the handmade from a young age. My mother was always making things, and as a result, I always had beautiful handmade clothes. It was from her that I learned to sew and embroider, and her love of the sewing arts made me want to study all things textile. I ended up taking a detour to study sculpture, pursue design, and teach at a secondary school, but in 2008 I needed a change, and stitching entered right back into my life where it belonged.

Question: Where do you stitch, and what projects are you typically working on?
ST: Now I construct objects by hand in my gingham armchair, with a cozy nest of fabrics and threads within easy reach. I create token jewelry treasures, charming little buttons, and anything else I can dream up with my needle and thread.

Question: What inspires your embroidery work?
ST: Nature is often my source of inspiration, and I am particularly smitten with birds. Give me fine embroidered details on a pretty bird and I'm a happy girl.

GATHER UP

Stitching Tool Kit (page 8)

Blackbird Sewing Kit motifs (next page)

¼ yard (.7 m) of evenweave gray linen or 16-count aida (see page 21)

¼ yard (.7 m) of gray patterned cotton

Scraps of green felt

14-count waste aida, 3 inches (7.6 cm) square

Six-strand embroidery floss, 1 skein each of yellow, turquoise, red, blue, metallic gold, brown, and black*

Sewing machine with zipper foot and standard foot

Gray zipper, at least 8 inches (20 cm) long

Batting, 7 x 12 inches (17.8 x 30.5 cm)

1½ yards (1.4 m) of double-fold green gingham bias binding, ¼ inch (6 mm) wide

The designer used DMC embroidery floss 307, 3846, 666, 312, E436, 810, and 310

Finished dimensions:
7½ x 4 inches (18.4 x10.2 cm) closed;
11½ x 7½ (29.2 x 19 cm) open

STITCHES YOU'LL USE

Holbein stitch (also known as Threaded running stitch)

Cross stitch (full, three-quarters, and variations, see page 20)

Straight stitch (also known as Running stitch and Seed stitch)

Blackbird Sewing Kit

This cute tri-fold sewing kit holds everything you need to keep your sewing supplies organized and tidy.

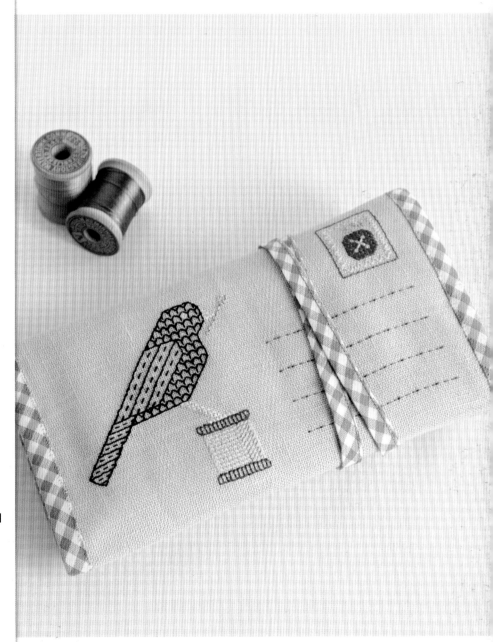

CUT THE FABRIC PIECES

1 From the evenweave gray linen or 160-count aida cloth, cut a piece that is 9 x 14 inches (22.9 x 35.6 cm). If you can't quite get 9 inches (22.9 cm) from the yardage, don't worry; the fabric will be trimmed down after embroidering.

2 From the gray patterned cotton, cut the following pieces:
- ▶ Main (cut 1): 7 x 12 inches (17.8 x 30.5 cm)
- ▶ Zip pocket (cut 1): 10 x 8 inches (25.4 x 20.3 cm)
- ▶ Slot pocket (cut 1): 8 inches (20.3 cm) square

3 From the green felt, cut the following pieces:
- ▶ Needle keeper (cut 2): 2½ inches (6.4 cm) square
- ▶ Mini safety pin cushion (cut 1 each): 1½ inches (3.8 cm) square, 1¼ inches (3.2 cm) square

STITCH ALONG

1 Place the linen or aida cloth onto your work surface with short sides on the top and bottom. Visualize it being divided into thirds. The center third is where the embroidery will go. Measure to find the center third and use a hand-sewing needle and thread to make horizontal basting stitches across the fabric. Also locate the exact center of the fabric and mark the spot with a pair of vertical and horizontal basting stitches.

2 Secure the linen in an embroidery hoop and embroider the blackbird, spool, horizontal lines, and postage stamp motifs according to the stitch guide. Make sure to work the design counting from the exact center and then outward so that you do not run out of fabric (see Cross Stitch Basics, page 20).

3 When the embroidery is complete, remove the piece from the hoop and carefully cut and remove the basting thread. Press the linen on the back side and trim the fabric to measure 7 x 12 inches (17.8 x 30.5 cm), keeping the center third centered.

4 Place the zip pocket cotton piece onto your work surface with the long sides on the top and bottom. Place the waste aida at the center, slightly toward the top of the piece and baste it in place with a hand-sewing needle and thread. Secure this section in an embroidery hoop and embroider the "sew" motif according to the stitch guide.

5 Take the finished piece out of the hoop. Remove the basting thread and trim away excess waste aida. Soak the piece in warm water for 5 to 10 minutes to loosen the waste aida and use tweezers to pull out any residual strands. Lay out the fabric flat to dry, then press the piece on the back side with an iron. Trim the piece to measure 8 x 4¾ inches (20.3 x 12 cm).

SEW ALONG

1 If you are working with a zipper that is longer than 8 inches (20.3 cm), follow manufacturer's instructions to shorten the zipper as needed. With right sides together, pin one long side of the zipper to the top edge of the embroidered zip pocket cotton piece. With the zipper foot attached to your sewing machine, stitch in place with a seam allowance of ¾ inch (1.9 cm). Make sure that the embroidery remains centered.

2 Spray one side of the batting with fabric spray adhesive and adhere the wrong side of the main cotton piece on top of the batting. Place this piece right side up on your work surface with short sides on the top and bottom.

3 Attach the zip pocket:
- ▶ Measure 3½ inches (8.9 cm) up from the bottom short end and mark with a pin on both side edges.
- ▶ With right sides together, center and pin the unstitched side of the zipper across the main fabric at this location. Stitch the zipper in place all the way across.
- ▶ Turn the zip pocket over so the wrong side is flat against the main cotton piece and the embroidery is facing up. Remove the zipper foot from your sewing machine and attach the standard foot.
- ▶ Pin and machine-baste around the edge of the pocket and true up any excess fabric to the main cotton piece.

4 Attach the slot pocket:

- ▸ Fold the slot pocket piece in half with short sides aligned and wrong sides together, and press.
- ▸ Tuck each short end to the inside by ⅜ inch (9.5 mm) and press.
- ▸ With the zip pocket to the right and the raw edges of the slot pocket aligned with the bottom raw edge of the main cotton piece, center and pin the slot pocket on the main piece, centered between the left edge of the main piece and the zipper.
- ▸ Stitch the right side of the slot pocket in place, getting as close

to the edge of the pocket as possible. Repeat for the left side.

5 Stitch additional lines on the pocket as follows:

- ▸ Stitch these additional vertical lines measured from the left edge as follows (see next page):
  - A: ¼ inch (6 mm)
  - B: 3¼ inches (8.3 cm)
  - C: 3½ inches (8.9 cm)
  - D: 5½ inches (14 cm)
  - E: 6½ inches (16.5 cm)
  - F: 7¾ inches (19.7 cm)
- ▸ For the scissor pocket, use a water-soluble marker to make a dot in the middle of the

space between lines C and D, approximately ½ inch (1.3 cm) up from the bottom edge. Stitch diagonally from each top edge to the marked point. Use a damp cloth to dab and remove the dot.

- ▸ True up any excess material from the slot pocket.

Sami Says

- ▸ I used two strands of floss for all embroidery stitches.

Blackbird Sewing Kit Motifs

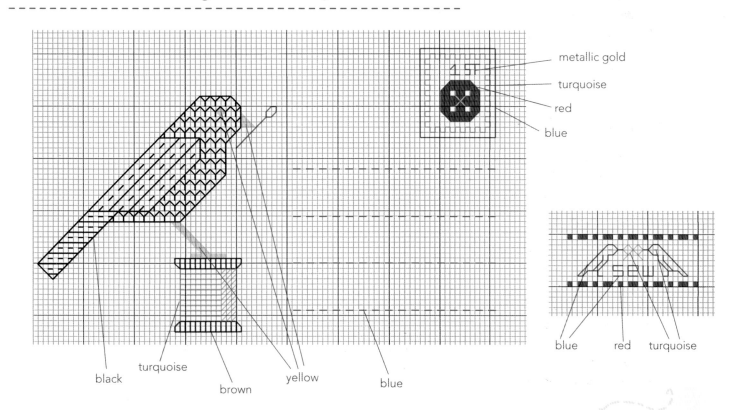

metallic gold
turquoise
red
blue

black
turquoise
brown
yellow
blue

blue   red   turquoise

6 Stack the two needle keeper felt squares and pin them above the slot pocket, toward the left edge. Sew diagonally through all thicknesses.

7 For the mini safety pin cushion, tack the larger felt square on top of the smaller felt square and pin them above the scissor pocket. Check that the position of the squares will allow the kit to comfortably fold in thirds. Stitch all four sides of the padded square felt, as close to the edges as possible.

8 Turn the main piece over and lay the embroidered panel on top of that with right sides facing. Pin and baste around all four sides.

9 Turn the layers over again with the embroidery side up. Pin and baste the bias binding along each edge, taking care to miter-fold each corner (see The Ties that Bind, page 13). Sew the binding, taking care to reinforce the zipper ends. Remove all basting stitches.

10 Make and attach the ties:
▸ Cut a 12-inch (30.5 cm) length of bias binding and stitch along its length to make ties.
▸ Turn up approximately ¼ inch (6 mm) at both ends and stitch.
▸ Fold the tie in half and pin it to the kit on the bias binding along the zipper pocket edge, toward the lower third of the edge.
▸ Take a 12-inch (30.5 cm) length of the bias binding, fold together along the center, and sew lengthwise. Turn up approximately ¼ inch (6 mm) at both ends and sew the ends shut. Fold this tie in half and sew it to the kit on the bias binding toward the lower third of the edge closest to the zipper pocket.

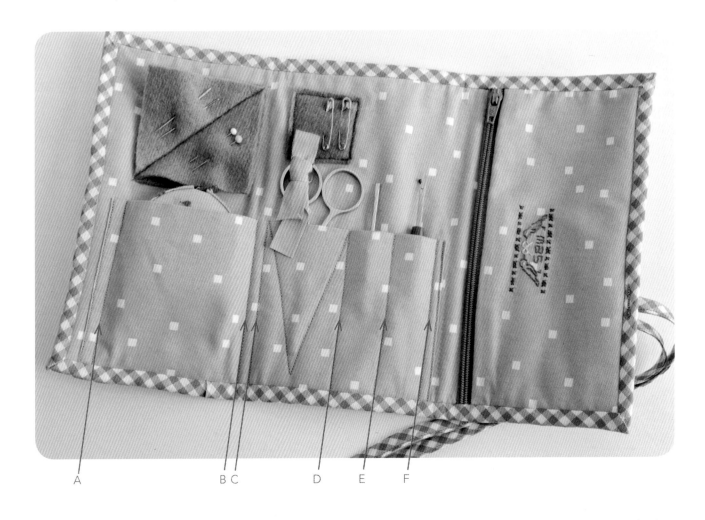

A   B C   D   E   F

Pincushion Brooch

Batting is what gives this faux button brooch its puffiness—a fun fashion accessory that can also serve double duty as a pincushion!

STITCH ALONG

1 The button motif (dashed circle with two dots, next page) is shown actual size; 1½ inches (3.8 cm) in diameter. Enlarge or reduce the motif as desired. Transfer it to the right side of the yellow gingham fabric.

2 With two buttonhole dots oriented vertically, place the piece of waste aida to the right of the buttonholes on the right side of the gingham fabric, making sure that it extends slightly over the transferred circle motif. Hand-baste the waste aida in place.

3 Secure the gingham with the basted waste aida in an embroidery hoop. Embroider the ladybug according to the stitch guide (next page). (See Cross Stitch Basics on page 20.)

4 Remove the basting thread and trim away excess waste aida that is blocking the button motif (the rest will be removed in step 6).

5 Embroider the remainder of the motif—the circle and two buttonhole dots—according to the stitch guide.

6 Remove the piece from the embroidery hoop and soak it in warm water for 5 to 10 minutes to loosen and remove the waste aida. This process will also remove any residual transfer lines as well. Use tweezers to pull out any residual strands of waste aida. Lay the fabric flat to dry, then press on the back side with an iron.

SEW ALONG

1 Use the small circle template to cut the following:
- ► 4 circles from the batting
- ► 2 circles from the firm white interfacing
- ► 1 circle from the fusible web

2 Use the large circle template to cut 1 circle from the backing fabric.

3 Make the pin backing:
- ► Follow manufacturer's instructions and use the fusible web circle to fuse one of the interfacing circles to the back side of the backing fabric circle, making sure that the interfacing is centered on the backing fabric.
- ► Hand-sew the pin back to the right side of the backing fabric, slightly above the center.
- ► Cut a piece of scrap fabric large enough to cover the sewn pin back and whipstitch in place with gray perle cotton (or other coordinating color). If you have a personal fabric label, this is a good place to use it.

GATHER UP

Stitching Tool Kit (page 8)
Button motif (next page)
Ladybug motif (next page)
Yellow gingham cotton fabric, 4 inches (10.2 cm) square or slightly larger to fit into embroidery hoop
14-count waste aida, 2 inches (5.1 cm) square
Six-strand embroidery floss, 1 skein each of red, and black*
Small container of warm water
Tweezers
Circle templates (next page)
Piece of batting, 12 x 3 inches (30.5 x 7.6 cm)
Piece of firm white interfacing, 6 x 3 inches (15.2 x 7.6 cm)
Fusible web, 3 inches (7.6 cm) square
Patterned fabric scrap for backing, 3 inches (7.6 cm) square
Perle cotton (size 8), 1 skein each of gray, and yellow
Pin back

The designer used DMC embroidery floss 666, and 310

Finished dimensions: 2 inches (5.1 cm) in diameter

STITCHES YOU'LL USE

Holbein stitch (also known as Threaded running stitch)
Satin stitch
Cross stitch (full, three-quarter, and variations, see page 20)

4 Assemble the pin front:
- ▸ Place the gingham embroidered fabric right side down onto your work surface and trim the four corners with scissors.
- ▸ Stack and place the four batting circles in the center of the gingham. Onto this stack, place the remaining interfacing circle.
- ▸ Use your hands to push down the stack of circles as you fold over the raw edges of the gingham and pin them over the pressed layers of batting and interfacing, making sure that the embroidered motif stays centered. Trim excess fabric.

5 Sew the pin front to the pin backing:
- ▸ Pin the fused backing fabric to the pinned gingham, tucking under excess backing fabric and making sure that the pin back is placed where you would like it to be.
- ▸ Whipstitch the backing fabric to the gingham with yellow perle cotton, removing pins as you go.

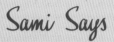

Sami Says

- ▸ I used two strands of floss on all embroidery stitches.
- ▸ Instead of a pin back, convert this into a bracelet pincushion. Use the whipstitch to attach a length of elastic large enough to fit on your wrist.

Pincushion Brooch Motif & Templates

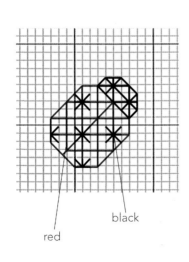

red

black

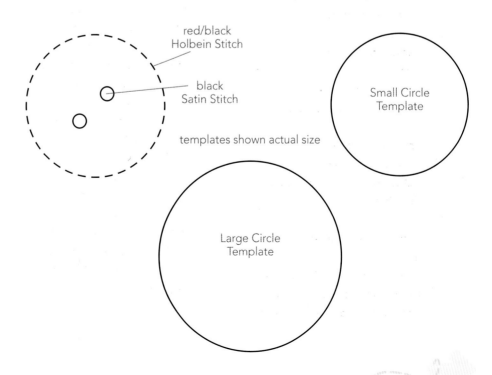

red/black
Holbein Stitch

black
Satin Stitch

templates shown actual size

Small Circle
Template

Large Circle
Template

Embroidered Buttons

You can make the cutest buttons with just a bit of aida cloth and basic cross stitch patterns.

GATHER UP

Stitching Tool Kit (page 8)

Embroidered Buttons motifs
(next page)

5 pieces of 16-count white
aida cloth, each 2 inches
(5.1 cm) square

Six-strand embroidery floss, 1
skein each of turquoise, red,
blue, and metallic gold*

Interfacing

5 aluminum covered-button kits,
⅞ inch (2.2 cm) size

*The designer used DMC
embroidery floss 3846, 666,
312, and E436*

Finished dimensions: ⅞ inch
(2.2 cm) diameter, each button

STITCHES
YOU'LL USE

Cross stitch (full, three-quarter,
and variations, see page 20)

STITCH ALONG

1 Embroider a button motif onto each of the cut aida pieces. Be sure to find the center of each piece of cloth by folding it in half vertically and then in half horizontally. Mark the center with your needle and start with the stitch closest to the center and continue from there.

2 Trim an embroidered square of aida into a circle that is approximately 1½ inches (3.8 cm) in diameter. Trim a piece of interfacing into a circle the same size. Place the embroidered aida onto your work surface, embroidered side down. Place the interfacing on top of the aida, on the wrong side.

3 Following manufacturer's instructions, sandwich the aida and interfacing layers between the two-part aluminum buttons and snap together.

4 Repeat steps 1 to 3 for the other button motifs.

Project Notes

▸ Buy enough kits to make five buttons, one for each button motif.
▸ There is no need to size or transfer motifs for this project. Simply use the motifs provided below, designed to be used with 16-count aida cloth, and go by the Cross Stitch Basics (page 20), to make your embroidery stitches.

Sami Says

▸ I used two strands of floss on all stitches.
▸ If you want a little bit of metallic shimmer on all five buttons, you can use the metallic gold floss for certain motif elements in the other three buttons.
▸ For a more unified look, select just one button motif and just one or two colors of floss and make all five buttons exactly the same.

Embroidered Buttons Motifs

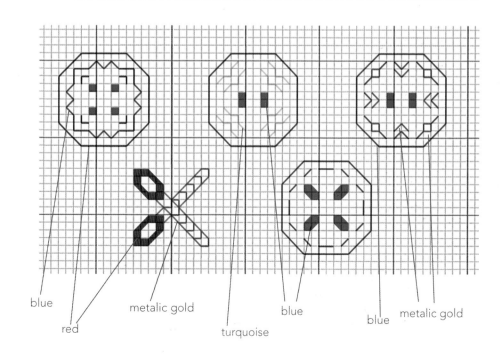

blue

red

metalic gold

turquoise

blue

blue

metalic gold

from the heart
stitch along with *Rebecca Sower*

photo: Kimberly Mahr

rebecca elevates the ordinary

Rebecca's intricate, beautiful work speaks to me, and every time I look at her pieces I notice another fantastic detail. I love that she uses exquisite stitches even in her flowers and hearts, thereby elevating even the simplest of shapes. Her color palettes are beautifully thought out and her addition of things like buttons and letters complement her stitches perfectly. Stitch along with Rebecca to discover how to make every stitch special and lovely.

— Jenny Doh

Question: Where did you first learn to stitch?

RS: I spent most of my young years at the feet of my seamstress grandmother, learning stitches and watching her work magic with her sewing machine. She taught me that the mere pull of a needle through a piece of cloth can be therapeutic, and to this day, stitching brings back fond memories of that time shared with her.

Question: How does the art of stitching fit into the vision you have for your life?

RS: I'm a big believer in living a handcrafted life. There is much joy and reward in using my hands to bring beauty, comfort, and love to my home and family, and stitching is one of the most tangible ways I do this.

Question: Why do you think the art of stitching has stood the test of time?

RS: There is something about stitching that all the factories in the world cannot take away from us—it's the connection that we feel with other stitchers who have practiced their art over the centuries. Once you've made your first hand-stitched piece, you connect with like-minded crafters. Specific handcrafts may fall from popularity over time, but creating something with our hands and a simple piece of thread will never leave us. It's part of who we are down to our souls.

Love Sachet

This is a great project for using your favorite stash fabric pieces. Place the final sachet in your lingerie drawer or leave it out on your night stand to enjoy the scent and the stitches.

STITCH ALONG

1 The motif (next page) is shown actual size; approximately 4 x 4¾ inches (10.2 x 12 cm). Enlarge or reduce the motif as desired.

2 Cut a piece of interfacing to measure slightly larger than the size of the motif. Center the interfacing on the back side of the linen, and follow manufacturer's instructions to fuse it to the linen with an iron.

3 Transfer the motif (see page 10) onto the center front of the cream linen.

4 Transfer the large heart in the upper left portion of the house onto the small scrap of pink floral quilting cotton and trim the fabric into the shape of a heart, slightly larger than the

transferred image. Use fabric spray adhesive to attach the scrap fabric to the cream linen, aligning the large hearts. This does not have to be perfectly aligned, just generally so.

5 Secure the linen in an embroidery hoop and embroider according to the stitch guide, making note of the following:
- Start with the scrap fabric heart and embroider through both fabric layers.
- For the beaded heart, thread a beading needle with one strand of red embroidery floss and start from the bottom point of the heart by pulling up the floss from the back side of the linen to the front side. Add approximately 4 to 5 seed beads to the floss and then

GATHER UP

Stitching Tool Kit (page 8)

Love Sachet motif (next page)

1 piece of cream linen, 7½ x 8 inches (19 x 20.3 cm)

Lightweight fusible interfacing

1 small scrap of pink floral quilting cotton

Fabric spray adhesive

Six-strand embroidery floss, 1 skein each of red and pink

Perle cotton (size 8), 1 skein each of pale yellow, brown, pale pink, and dark pink

Beading needle

Dark red seed beads (approximately 70–80)

1 piece of white cotton, slightly larger than the cream linen piece

1 piece of floral quilting cotton, slightly larger than the white cotton piece

1 piece of white linen, slightly smaller than the floral quilting cotton piece

Sewing machine with standard foot

1 cup of dried lavender buds (or other dried potpourri)

Vintage millinery flower with stem (or other silk flower with stem)

Finished dimensions: 7 x 8½ inches (17.8 x 21.6 cm)

STITCHES YOU'LL USE

Back stitch

Chain stitch

Cross stitch

Running stitch (also known as Straight stitch and Seed stitch)

Satin stitch

anchor the beads by pushing the needle down through the linen. Pull the needle back up from the back side, very close to the last piercing. Add another 4 to 5 seed beads. Repeat until you have completed the beaded heart. Take the embroidered linen from the hoop and remove any transfer lines as needed (see page 12).

6 Place the embroidered linen on top of the white cotton piece, then on top of the floral quilting cotton, and then on top of the white linen piece. Pin the layers together and use a sewing machine to straight stitch along all edges with approximately a ⅜-inch (9.5 mm) seam allowance, leaving a 2-inch (5.1 cm) gap along the bottom

edge. Be sure to backstitch at the start and end points.

7 Fill the sachet with dried lavender buds through the gap at the bottom edge, between the white cotton and floral quilting cotton. Machine-stitch the opening closed. Zigzag-stitch along all four sides again, directly above the straight stitch lines.

8 Attach a vintage millinery flower piece to the front of the sachet by couch stitching the stem with six strands of pink embroidery floss.

Love Sachet Motif

shown actual size

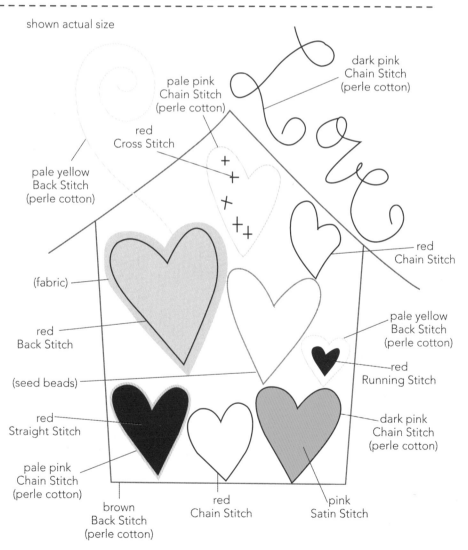

dark pink
Chain Stitch
(perle cotton)

pale pink
Chain Stitch
(perle cotton)

red
Cross Stitch

pale yellow
Back Stitch
(perle cotton)

red
Chain Stitch

(fabric)

red
Back Stitch

pale yellow
Back Stitch
(perle cotton)

(seed beads)

red
Running Stitch

red
Straight Stitch

dark pink
Chain Stitch
(perle cotton)

pale pink
Chain Stitch
(perle cotton)

brown
Back Stitch
(perle cotton)

red
Chain Stitch

pink
Satin Stitch

Rebecca Says

▶ I used six strands of floss to fill the heart on the bottom right corner. I used two strands of floss for all other stitches where I used floss, and then perle cotton on everything else, as noted.

▶ Old bed sheets, pillowcases, and dishtowels provide good options for fabrics that can be cut up to make this project.

Love Journal

After all the hand embroidery, free-motion stitching will tie everything together for this journal cover, giving it lots of depth and texture. If you want to keep it lighter, you can decide not to add the free-motion stitching. It's up to you!

GATHER UP

Stitching Tool Kit (page 8)

Love Journal motif (page 87)

Assorted scraps of vintage linens and lace

Linen fabric, 27 x 12 inches (68.6 x 30.5 cm)

Six-strand embroidery floss, pale yellow, brown, dark yellow, mustard, pale green, white, teal, peach, medium green, light green, cream, and rust

Sewing machine with darning foot and standard foot

1 quarter (coin)

Thin cardboard

Small vintage mother-of-pearl buttons

1 yard (.9 m) of light green seam tape (or other ribbon)

Composition notebook, 7½ x 9¾ inches (19 x 24.8 cm)

Finished dimensions: 7½ x 9¾ inches (19 x 24.8 cm)

STITCHES YOU'LL USE

Back stitch

Chain stitch

Cross stitch

French knot

Lazy daisy

Satin stitch

Straight stitch (also known as Running stitch and Seed stitch)

STITCH ALONG

1 Cut the scrap fabrics as follows, then set them aside:
  ▸ Scrap #1 (lace), 2 x 1 inches (5.1 x 2.5 cm)
  ▸ Scrap #2 (white linen), 1¼ x 1¾ inches (3.2 x 9.5 cm)
  ▸ Scrap #3 (white linen), approximately 2¼ x 4 inches (5.7 x 10.2 cm)

2 Size the motif (page 87) to measure slightly smaller than 7¾ x 9½ inches (19.7 x 24.1 cm).

3 Only the cover portion of the linen will be embroidered. To prepare the cover:
  ▸ Place the linen on your work surface with the long sides at the top and bottom. Fold it in half from left to right so that the fold is on the left side and the other sides are raw edges. Press.
  ▸ Cut a piece of interfacing to measure slightly larger than the size of the motif.
  ▸ Open the linen (like you would open a book). Position the interfacing on the left side with one edge along the fold and centered top to bottom. Follow manufacturer's instructions to fuse it to the linen with an iron.
  ▸ Refold the linen so that the fold is on the left side.
  ▸ Transfer the motif (see page 10) onto the right side of the linen, lined up with the interfacing on the wrong side.

4 Secure the linen in an embroidery hoop and embroider according to the stitch guide shown, making note of the following:

  ▸ Incorporate scrap #1 on the upper left and embroider through both thicknesses on all sides of the lace.
  ▸ Incorporate scrap #2 near the bottom edge and embroider through both thicknesses on all sides of the linen.
  ▸ Prepare scrap #3 with appliqued circles (next page) to be machine-stitched on the upper right section in step 6.

5 Prepare your sewing machine for free-motion stitching by lowering the machine's feed dogs and attaching the darning foot. Stitch small circles in the non-embroidered sections of the linen. Do as little or as much as you like.

6 With the machine still in free-motion stitching mode, stitch the prepared scrap #3 to the upper right section of the piece. Hand-sew the small mother-of-pearl buttons onto the lower portion, through all thicknesses. Replace the darning foot on your sewing machine with the standard foot.

7 With two strands of teal floss, add running stitches along all sides of the journal cover to "frame" the embroidery.

SEW ALONG

1 With the embroidered side facing down, press under the short sides by ½ inch (1.3 cm) and use a sewing machine to stitch down both sides.

2 Press under the bottom long edge by ¼ inch (6 mm) and stitch across. Press under the top long edge by ¼ inch (6 mm), but before sewing this edge, fold the seam tape in half and tuck the folded short edge at the center fold. Stitch across, making sure to catch the seam tape.

3 To make the cover pocket flaps:

- ▸ Fold back and press the finished short edges by 5½ inches (14 cm) so that right sides are touching.
- ▸ Stitch a ⅝ inch (1.6 cm) seam along the top and bottom edges of both folded section.
- ▸ Clip threads and trim corners diagonally to alleviate bulk.
- ▸ Turn the cover pocket flaps right side out and press, making sure to press the top and bottom center edges ⅝ inch (1.6 cm) to align with the stitched flaps. Stitch these center edges.

4 Fold back the composition book covers and insert them into the fabric cover pocket flaps. Close the journal.

Appliqued Circles

The scrap #3 rectangle is a nice textural addition to the journal cover. Here are the steps for preparing it:

1 Start by embroidering small straight stitches on the upper two-thirds with two strands of mustard embroidery floss.

2 On a scrap piece of tan linen, use a quarter (coin) to trace two circles with a nonpermanent marker. Use one strand of white embroidery floss to embroider small cross stitches in one circle and four rows of zigzag patterned back stitches in the second circle. Use two strands of mustard floss to make small cross stitches on the second circle.

3 Trace the quarter onto thin cardboard (like a cereal box) and cut it out to make a template. Set it aside.

4 Cut the first circle from the linen with an added ¼-inch (6 mm) along the circumference for seam allowance. With a hand-sewing needle and thread, make a row of straight stiches ⅛ inch (3 mm) from the edge of the fabric circle.

5 Place the cardboard template on the wrong side of the fabric circle and pull up the thread so the fabric folds up and onto the template. Tie the thread ends and press both sides. Let the fabric cool and then remove the thread and template.

6 Repeat steps 4 and 5 for the second circle.

7 Appliqué both circles onto the upper two-thirds of the white linen piece, using a blind stitch. Leave room toward the bottom of scrap #3 to attach buttons later.

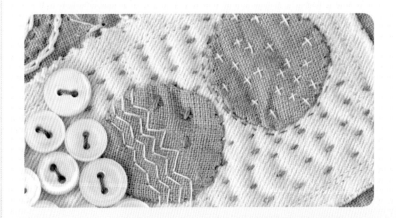

Love Journal Motif

enlarge 150%

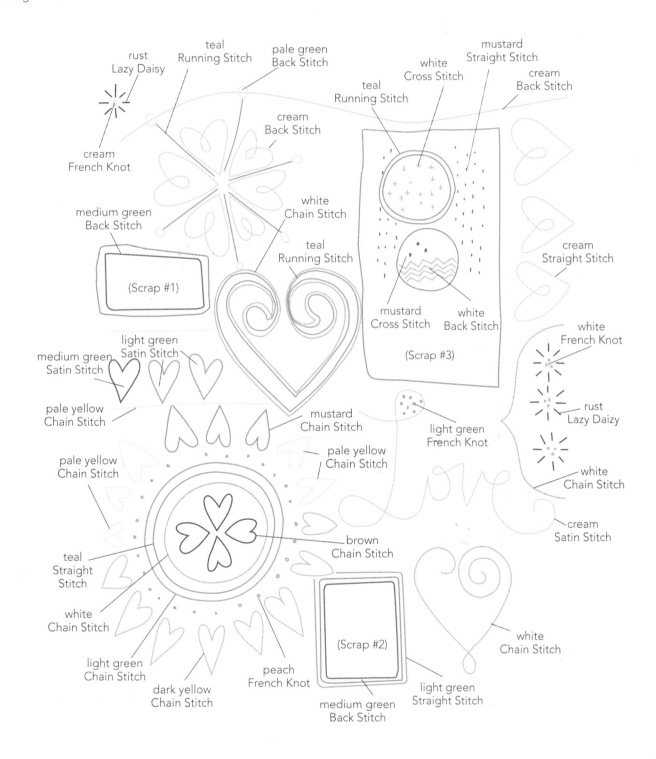

GATHER UP

Stitching Tool Kit (page 8)

Love Wall Art motif (next page)

Lightweight fusible interfacing

1 piece of heavy canvas cloth,
    6 x 7 inches (15.2 x 17.8 cm)

Six-strand embroidery floss, 1 skein
    each of brown, dark pink, white, light
    green, orange, coral, and pale pink

Craft glue

Scrap cardboard (or matboard),
    slightly smaller than 4½ x 6 inches
    (11.4 x 15.2 cm)

Frame without glass, 12 inches
    (30.5 cm) square

White spray paint (optional)

Plywood to fit the back of the frame

8 small nails

Hammer

1–2 sheets of vintage sheet music
    (or other patterned paper)

Gel medium

Finished dimensions: the embroidery
is 6 x 7 inches (15.2 x 17.8 cm), the
frame is 12 inches (30.5 cm) square

STITCHES YOU'LL USE

Back stitch

Bullion stitch

Cross stitch (see page 20)

French knot

Lazy daisy stitch

Satin stitch

Straight stitch (also known as
    Running stitch and Seed stitch)

Love Wall Art

Use a second-hand frame to display your embroidered work in a way that is unique, eye-catching, and affordable.

STITCH AND FRAME ALONG

1 The motif (next page) is shown actual size; approximately 4 x 5 inches (10.2 x 12.7 cm).

2 Cut a piece of interfacing to measure slightly larger than the size of the motif. Center the interfacing on the back side of the canvas cloth, and follow manufacturer's instructions to fuse it to the cloth with an iron.

3 Transfer the motif (see page 10) onto the center front of the canvas cloth.

4 Without placing the fabric in a hoop, embroider according to the stitch guide. The canvas cloth with fused interfacing will be thick and stable enough to embroider without a hoop. Remove any transfer lines as needed (see page 12).

5 Trim the piece with scissors to measure 4½ x 6 inches (11.4 x 15.2 cm).

6 Use craft glue to adhere the embroidered cloth onto the cardboard or matboard. Let it dry.

7 If your frame is not white and you want white, paint it with white spray paint and let it dry.

8 Use a hammer and nails to attach the plywood to the back side of the frame.

9 With th
facing y
the plyw
frame w
fingers
air bubb

Love

shown actual

dark
Straight

coral
Lazy Daizy

pale pink
Satin Stitch

dark pink
Satin Stitch

dark pink
French Knot

light green
Satin Stitch

dark pink
Buillion Stitch

pale pink
French Knot

light green
Lazy Daizy

dark pink
Satin Stitch

white
Back Stitc

Elegant Seahorse Napkin

For your next sea-themed dinner party, embroider a set of napkins that will impress your guests. Go the extra mile, if you like, by embroidering other sea-themed motifs by Nicole (page 124) on a large, plain white tablecloth.

GATHER UP

Stitching Tool Kit (page 8)
Elegant Seahorse Napkin motif
1 white cotton fabric napkin,
   14½ inches (36.8 cm) square
Six-strand embroidery floss, 1 skein
   each of rust, pale peach, and
   bright blue

Finished dimensions: 14½ inches
(36.8 cm) square

STITCHES YOU'LL USE

Back stitch
French knot

STITCH ALONG

1 Size the Seahorse motif (below) to approximately 4 inches (10.2 cm) tall.

2 Transfer the motif (see page 10) diagonally onto one of the corners of the napkin.

3 Secure the napkin in an embroidery hoop, centering the motif, and embroider according to the stitch guide shown.

4 Take the finished piece out of the hoop and remove any transfer lines as needed (see page 12).

5 Repeat these steps to make additional embroidered napkins as desired.

Elegant Seahorse Motif

shown actual size

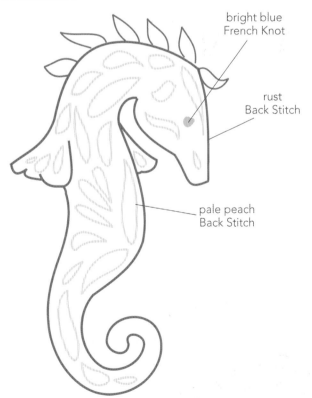

bright blue French Knot

rust Back Stitch

pale peach Back Stitch

Nicole Says

▸ The outline of the seahorse was done with four strands of floss.
▸ The inner part of the seahorse was done with two strands of floss.
▸ The eye was made with three strands of floss.

Polar Bear in Newspaper Boat Dress

Whether you make the girl's dress or buy one, you can add to its beauty by embroidering this sweet motif with just a few shades of coordinating floss.

GATHER UP

Stitching Tool Kit (page 8)

Polar Bear in Newspaper Boat motif (below)

Little girl's dress made in white cotton fabric*

Six-strand embroidery floss, 1 skein each of dark aqua, aqua, and pale aqua**

Nicole used a freebie Oliver+S pattern called the popover sundress. Look for it by going to http://oliverands.com, and clicking on "free patterns."

**If the dress you buy or make has trim in shades other than aqua, select colors that will coordinate with the dress trim.*

Finished dimensions: fits a 2- to 3-year old girl

STITCHES YOU'LL USE

Back stitch

Satin stitch

Straight stitch (also known as Running stitch and Seed stitch)

STITCH ALONG

1 Imagine the motif below (including the seagulls, boat with bear, and water) as fitting within a circle and size it to approximately a 4½-inch (11.4 cm) in diameter.

2 Transfer the motif (see page 10) onto the lower left front of the dress. Secure that portion of the dress in an embroidery hoop and embroider according to the stitch guide.

3 Take the dress out of the hoop and remove any transfer lines as needed (see page 12).

Nicole Says

▸ The eyes and nose of the bear were stitched with two strands of floss.

▸ The outline of the photos, waves, and birds were stitched with three strands of floss.

▸ Everything else was stitched with four strands of floss.

▸ I chose a cool blue/aqua palette to complement the blue/aqua in the dress I was stitching on, but I think this pattern would also work very well in a black/gray/white palette.

Polar Bear in Newspaper Boat Motif

shown actual size

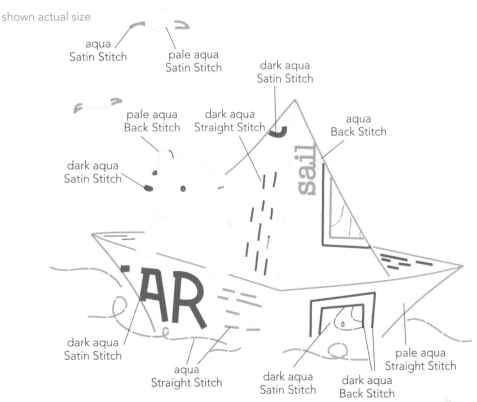

Sea Bird Wall Art

This elegant bird is made with lots and lots of straight stitches that mimic the direction of the bird's feathers. The stitches vary in lengths and colors, which add to the subtle beauty of the design.

GATHER UP

Stitching Tool Kit (page 8)
Sea Bird motif (next page)
3-inch (7.6 cm) embroidery hoop
1 piece of batting, 5 inches (12.7 cm) square
1 piece of blue/green quilting cotton, 5 inches (12.7 cm) square
Six-strand embroidery floss, 1 skein each of white, light gray, dark gray, pale pink, black, orange, and blue-green
Fabric spray adhesive
Mod Podge
10 inches (25.4 cm) of lace ribbon, 1 inch (2.5 cm) wide

Finished dimensions: 3 inches (7.6 cm) in diameter

STITCHES YOU'LL USE

Long and short stitch
Straight stitch (also known as Running stitch and Seed stitch)

STITCH ALONG

1 Imagine the motif below (including the bird, the clouds, and water) as fitting within a circle, and size it to approximately a 2-inch (5.1 cm) diameter.

2 Use the inner section of the wooden hoop to trace a circle onto the batting and cut out the circle. Check that it will fit inside the hoop and trim as needed. Set aside.

3 Center and transfer the motif (see page 10) onto the front of the quilting cotton. Secure the fabric in a wooden embroidery hoop and embroider according to the stitch guide.

4 Take the finished piece out of the hoop and remove any transfer lines as needed (see page 12). When the fabric is dry, gently press and secure it back onto the embroidery hoop, center the motif, with the metal closure at the top (it will be used later for hanging).

5 Apply fabric spray adhesive onto one side of the cut batting from step 2. Adhere the batting to the back side of the embroidered work, inside the hoop.

6 Cut the fabric, leaving just enough to wrap around the back inside of the inner hoop. Fold over and glue this excess fabric to the inner hoop using Mod Podge. Let dry.

7 Thread the lace ribbon through the gap at the top of the hoop near the metal closure. Tie the ends at the top and use the ribbon as a hanger.

Nicole Says

▸ All stitches were made with two strands of floss.

▸ Start with the bird's body first, fill-stitching it with white floss. Make sure to leave irregular gaps to fill in with silver/gray floss. Note: When you are fill-stitching, remember to mimic the direction the feathers are going.

▸ Fill-stitch the wing area with the light gray floss and then add a few stitches under the tip of the wing with darker gray floss. Note: Do not completely fill-stitch the wing; allow some of the background fabric to show through.

▸ Vary the length of your fill stitches. For example, the tail looks better stitched with longer stitches while the stitches on the body, head, and beak look better with shorter stitches.

▸ In the darker parts of the tail, mix in a few lighter stitches to avoid the feathers looking too solid. Gradually increase the lighter stitches toward the base of the tail.

Sea Bird Wall Art Motif

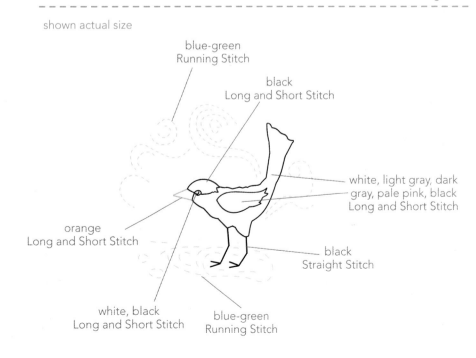

shown actual size

blue-green
Running Stitch

black
Long and Short Stitch

white, light gray, dark gray, pale pink, black
Long and Short Stitch

black
Straight Stitch

orange
Long and Short Stitch

white, black
Long and Short Stitch

blue-green
Running Stitch

doodle stitch along with *Pam Garrison*

photo: Johanna Love

pam doodles with needle and thread

Pam's creativity really shines through in her stitched projects. She combines simple shapes into lines of stitches that then form her overall designs. The heart of what she presents in her projects is based on her love of doodle stitching, which is a creation of traditional stitches combined with an inventive twist. Her stitches are sometimes exaggerated or modified so that the thread will do what she wants it to do, just the way you would want a pencil to make the marks you want it to make on paper. Stitch along with Pam to create your own inventive stitched pieces.

— Jenny Doh

Question: What do you enjoy about stitching?
PG: I love losing myself in the quiet, contemplative creativity that comes with stitching. There's something about getting lost in the colors, stitches, and textures of an embroidery piece that is just delightful. I also love that stitching is a great transportable medium to take on the go. I've even practiced my stitches sitting at a baseball tournament!

Question: When you sit down to stitch, what is your method?
PG: Sometimes I stick with simple stitches that I know by heart, and other times I enjoy the challenge of learning a new stitch and practicing it. No matter what I go with, I know that it will be uniquely mine— the beauty of embroidery is that the look and feel of the final product depends on the artist who is doing the stitching.

Question: Why do you think the art of stitching has risen in popularity recently?
PG: Stitching served an important purpose for centuries—people have always needed clothing and blankets, after all—but the Internet today allows us to see more inspirational and soulful stitching than ever before. There's no shortage of possibilities with stitching, and there is always joy in the process.

Arrow Pillow

The arrow motif is an ideal shape for an oblong pillow. Start the embroidery by making the outline stitches first and then filling in the shape with other stitches. Follow the stitch guide provided or use other stitches that you favor. It's up to you!

Doodle Stitches Sample Book

This no-sew book is made with pages of felt where you can practice stitching in freeform style. Put it all together with the help of a hot glue gun. Refer to the book to help remind you of your favorite stitches!

GATHER UP

Stitching Tool Kit (page 8)

Doodle Stitches Sample Book motif
  (page 105)

9 inches (22.9 cm) of wide green felt ribbon
  for the cover, 3¾ inches (9.5 cm) wide*

Vintage pinking machine (optional)

Scallop-edged fabric shears (optional)

9 x 12-inch (22.9 x 30.5 cm) sheets of wool
  felt or felt scraps for book pages, in
  white, beige, mustard, and brown

¼ yard (22.9 cm) of thin yellow wool fabric

Pinking shears

Six-strand embroidery floss and perle
  cotton (size 5), skeins in assorted colors**

Piece of linen, 7½ x 3½ inches (19 x 8.9 cm)

Vintage metallic thread or metallic
  embroidery floss (optional)

Hot glue gun and glue sticks

*If you are unable to find green velvet
  ribbon, cut regular velvet to size and trim
  all sides with pinking shears.*

**The purpose of this project is to make a
  booklet tailored to your favorite stitches
  and stitch colors. So gather as many
  different colors of floss and/or perle
  cotton as you like and use them to fill
  the pages.*

Finished dimensions: 4 x 4 x 1¼ inches
(10.2 x 10.2 x 3.2 cm)

STITCHES YOU'LL USE

Satin stitch

Your choice of additional stitches

STITCH ALONG THE COVER

1 Cut scallops along the short
  ends of the velvet ribbon with
  a vintage pinking machine
  and scallop-edged blade.
  Alternatively, use scallop-edged
  fabric shears or traditional
  pinking shears. The final trimmed
  piece should measure 8½ inches
  (21.6 cm) in length.

2 Place the velvet horizontally on
  your work surface with the wrong
  side facing you. Fold it in half
  with wrong sides touching and
  the two short scalloped edges on
  the right. The velvet facing you
  will be the front cover of the book
  where you stitch the title. In order
  to account for the spine, position
  the words so that the last letters
  of the two stacked words (doodle
  stitches) are ¾ inch (1.9 cm) from
  the right scalloped edge.

3 Either freeform stitch the title,
  "doodle stitches," or stitch
  through the tracing paper and
  velvet (see Hints for Stitching on
  Velvet) according to the stitch
  guide. Carefully tear away the
  tracing paper, making sure none
  of the embroidery is disturbed.
  Set the ribbon aside.

Hints for Stitching on Velvet

▸ Pam did not use an embroidery hoop for this project. The small
  felt pieces are stiff enough to hold in your hands while stitching.
  The velvet is not as stiff, but can still be handheld while stitched.

▸ Pam did not trace the title of the book on the velvet before
  stitching it, mainly because the velvet has so much texture. Pam
  visualized the words she wanted to stitch and did so in freeform
  style. If you would prefer not to freeform stitch, use the Doodle
  Stitches Sample Book motif (shown actual size on page 105;
  approximately 2½ x 2 inches [6.4 x 5.1 cm]), to trace it onto
  tracing paper, then pin the paper in place and stitch through the
  tracing paper and velvet according to the stitch guide.

STITCH ALONG THE PAGES

1 From the wool felt, cut the following pieces for book pages.

- ▸ 4 double-page pieces (2 white, 1 mustard, 1 brown): 6½ x 3½ inches (16.5 x 8.9 cm)
- ▸ 2 single-page pieces (beige): 3¼ x 3½ inches (8.3 x 8.9 cm)

From the thin yellow wool felt fabric, cut and piece enough 2-inch (5.1 cm) wide strips to make one continuous 20-inch (50.8 cm) long strip.

2 Trim both short edges of the 4 double-page pieces with pinking shears or scallop-edged fabric shears. Trim only one 3½-inch (8.9 cm) edge of the single-page pieces. The trimmed sides will be the outer edges of each page.

3 Before embroidering, fold each double-page piece in half with trimmed edges aligned. Mark the center fold with a pin; this is where you will attach the pages to the book. When you embroider, leave ¼- to ½-inch (6 mm to 1.3 cm) margin on each side of the fold so your designs don't get lost. Leave the same margin on the untrimmed edge of the single page pieces.

4 Embroider the pages however you like. Pam stitched everything freeform style, and you are encouraged to do the same. These pages are intended to be a practice ground for your favorite embroidery stitches. If you would prefer not to freeform-stitch, use a nonpermanent fabric marker to plan words and designs, then use your marks as guides to embroider each page.

5 When finished, remove any marks or stray threads as necessary.

ASSEMBLE THE BOOK

There are three different ways you can assemble signatures for the book. (Signatures are a collection of pages that are sewn to the spine.) These instructions cover all three options.

1 The first way is to put together two embroidered double-page pieces with wrong sides facing and adhere them with a hot glue gun. This will hide the back side of the embroidery between the pages and form a 4-page signature.

2 The second way is to lay a double-page piece face down and, with wrong sides facing, lay down two single page pieces, aligning the outside trimmed edges. (This is a good fallback option if you're not happy with one of your double-page embroidered pieces. Just cut it in half, discard the half you don't like, and embroider another half piece.) Adhere the pages as before, back-to-back with a hot glue gun. This is also a 4-page signature.

3 The third way is to fold a double-page piece in half with wrong sides facing and glue the back sides together. This becomes a 2-page signature.

4 Instead of stitching the signatures directly to the cover (which would create lines of stitches on the spine of the book), you will sew the signatures to a strip of linen and glue the linen inside the book:

▸ Use pinking shears to trim all four sides of the 7½ x 3½-inch (19 x 8.9 cm) piece of linen.
▸ Fold the linen in half, aligning the short sides, and mark the center fold.
▸ Fold each of your 4-page signatures in half and make a stack of pages that includes the 2-page signature, in whatever order you like, aligning the trimmed outer edges.
▸ Take the center signature from the stack and pin its folded edge to the center fold of the linen strip. Pin the remaining signatures on both sides.
▸ Open each 4-page signature and hand-sew it to the linen with long running stitches. Hand-sew the 2-page signature with a whipstitch.

5 Finish the book:
▸ Fold the yellow ribbon tie in half, aligning short ends. Mark the center fold.

▸ Close all the signatures and wrap the linen around the pages. Wrap the ribbon tie around the pages, aligning the center of the tie with the stitches for the center signature.
▸ Use hot glue to attach the ribbon to the front and then the back portions of the linen.
▸ Center and wrap the green velvet

around the entire piece and secure with a hot glue gun.
▸ Make reverse V cuts on the ends of the yellow felt fabric and tie the ends to hold the book closed.

Doodle Stitches Sample Book Cover Motif

- -

shown actual size

Satin Stitch

doodle stitches

Doodle Butterfly

Gauze is tricky to stitch on, but provides an extremely sheer and dreamy quality to the finished project. The wire will help keep the shape of the butterfly but in a loose fashion, honoring the freeform nature of the doodle-stitched design.

GATHER UP

Stitching Tool Kit (page 8)
Doodle Butterfly motif (next page)
Butterfly template (next page)
White copy paper
Gauze, 12 x 10 inches
    (30.5 x 25.4 cm)
Six-strand embroidery floss: skeins
    in assorted colors
1½ yards (1.4 m) of 24-gauge
    craft wire
Wire cutters

Finished dimensions: 10 x 7 inches
(25.4 x 17.8 cm)

STITCHES YOU'LL USE

Back stitch
Blanket stitch (also known as
    Buttonhole stitch)
Chain stitch (and zigzag chain variation)
Closed blanket stitch (also known as
    Closed buttonhole stitch)
Cross stitch (see page 20)
Fly stitch
French knot
Lazy daisy stitch
Running stitch (also known as
    Straight stitch and Seed stitch)
Satin stitch
Star stitch
Stem stitch
Woven rose (also known as Woven
    spider web)

SEW AND STITCH ALONG

1 Copy or trace the template onto regular white copy paper. Tape the paper onto a window with a good light source. Tape the gauze on top of the paper. The light from the window should allow you to see the template through the gauze. Use a nonpermanent marker to gently make small dots to mark the outline of the butterfly. Small dots, rather than thick lines, will help maintain the integrity of the gauze.

2 Because the gauze is so delicate, do the embroidery without transferring the stitch motif or putting the gauze into an embroidery hoop. Simply set the gauze gently on your lap and embroider it, using the stitch guide as a visual reference. This freeform approach helps keep the loose feel of the butterfly. If some of your stitches end up being slightly larger or smaller in size, or if you are only able to fit in five running stitches instead of six, that's okay. The end result will be unique to your hand and your stitching style.

3 Cut the butterfly shape along the traced lines so that the dots are cut away. Discard the excess gauze.

4 Use the craft wire as if you are making a loose running stitch around the edge of the butterfly:

▶ Start from the point where the head meets the start of the right wing, then thread your way around the entire right wing, the lower body, then the entire left wing.

▶ Twist and bend the wire back up the extended wire to the top of the body, then back down and up again as many more times as you can with the wire. As you do this, anchor the wire through the gauze at the top and bottom parts of the body a few times. It will look sort of tangled and the gauze will start to fray, which is a good thing.

▶ Bury the start and end points of the wire by bending and tucking it into itself and/or the gauze. Clip any excess wire with wire cutters.

5 Poke the lower portion of the twisted wire into a potted plant.

Doodle Butterfly Motif and Template

enlarge 200%

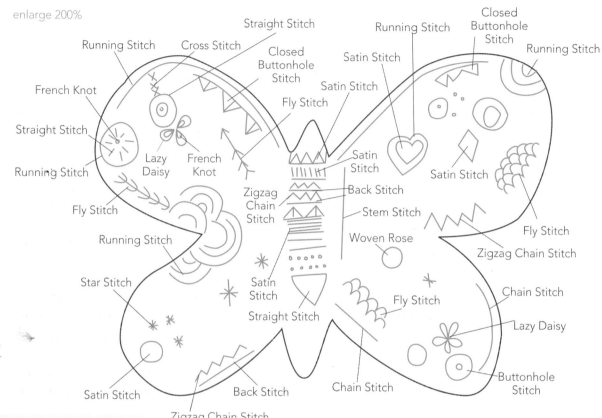

Running Stitch
French Knot
Straight Stitch
Running Stitch
Fly Stitch
Running Stitch
Star Stitch
Satin Stitch
Cross Stitch
Straight Stitch
Closed Buttonhole Stitch
Fly Stitch
Lazy Daisy
French Knot
Zigzag Chain Stitch
Satin Stitch
Straight Stitch
Back Stitch
Zigzag Chain Stitch
Running Stitch
Satin Stitch
Satin Stitch
Satin Stitch
Back Stitch
Stem Stitch
Woven Rose
Fly Stitch
Closed Buttonhole Stitch
Running Stitch
Satin Stitch
Fly Stitch
Zigzag Chain Stitch
Chain Stitch
Lazy Daisy
Chain Stitch
Buttonhole Stitch

Pam Says

▸ I used six strands of floss in assorted colors for all the floss embroidery.

▸ I used two strands of perle cotton for the blue flowers on the lower right wing and the upper left wing. All other perle cotton embroidery was done with a single strand of perle cotton.

▸ I think this project would be just as cute if stitched on a slightly heavier fabric.

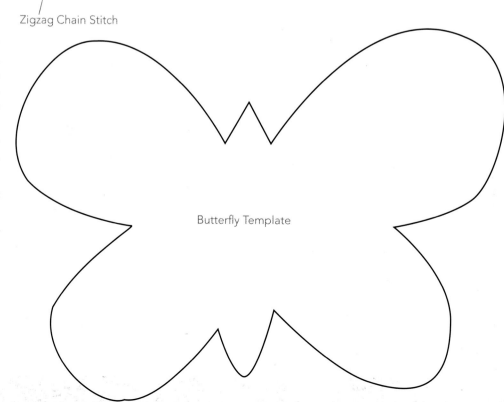

Butterfly Template

photo: Stephen R. Bowcutt

jackie stitches outside the box

I admire Jackie's ability to incorporate stitching into all of her art—you can see it in her sketchbooks, next to a painted patch of fabric, and even on a dyed tote bag. She really makes me think outside of the box when it comes to where I can use stitching in my daily art practice. Stitch along with Jackie to see how you can use stitching in your art projects— even if it's just as a detail.

—— Jenny Doh

Question: Have you always been a stitcher?

JB: I first learned to stitch in junior high school, but I took a break from it for many years. I came back to the art form via cross-stitched Christmas cards, and I haven't looked back since.

Question: Why do you like stitching?

JB: Stitching allows me to make work that is uniquely my own in a generally mass-produced world. It has opened my eyes to the world of art—to the pleasure of keeping a sketchbook, taking photographs, visiting exhibitions, and so much more. It's also relaxing, stimulating, and relatively inexpensive!

Question: Where do you typically work on your stitched projects?

JB: I stitch in a spare room that has become my overcrowded studio, with the most inspirational view out the window. I look out on an open field, which is ever shifting with the seasons. From newly harvested rows to green crop shoots, the field is always changing colors, which really pushes me to grow and think outside of the box with my art.

Catch Up Pouch

Three birds placed in a diagonal row look like they are climbing upward as they all try to catch up and reach their destination.

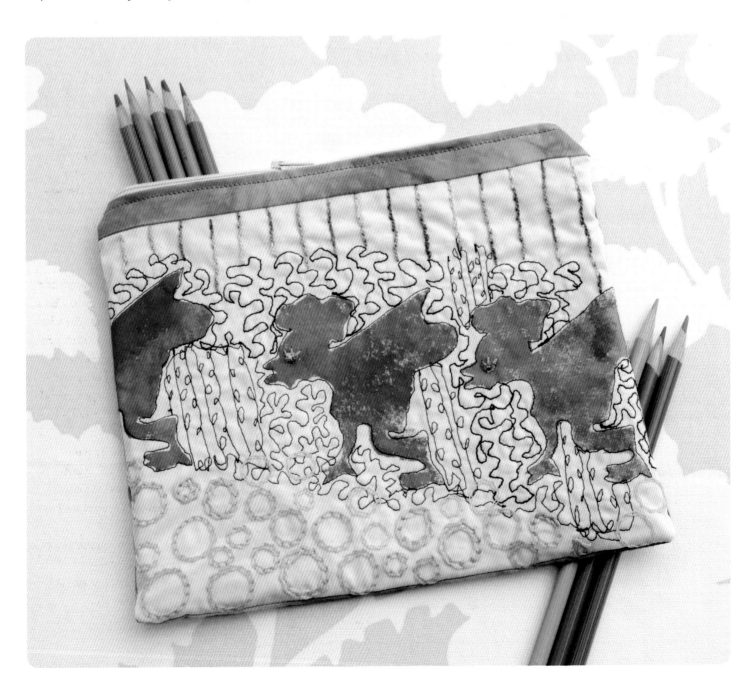

GATHER UP

Stitching Tool Kit (page 8)

Catch Up Pouch motif
(page 113)

1 sheet of plain white copy
paper

1 sheet of cardstock

Sharp craft knife

Masking tape

Softly padded work surface: for
example, a table with a large
piece of foam or a stack of
newspaper or layers of towels

1 piece of white cotton fabric
(front), 8½ x 7½ inches
(21.6 x 19 cm)

Ruler

Fabric paint, in two shades of
green

Palette

Stencil brush

Sewing machine with darning
foot, standard foot, and
zipper foot

Six-strand embroidery floss: 1
skein of lime green

Perle cotton (size 3), 1 skein of
variegated blue/green/yellow

2 small seed beads

2 pieces of top edge fabric in
contrasting color, 1¼ x 8½
inches (3.2 x 19 cm)

1 piece of backing fabric,
8½ x 7½ inches
(21.6 x 19 cm)

2 pieces of fusible webbing,
8½ x 8¼ inches
(19 x 21 cm)

Zipper, 9 inches
(22.9 cm) long

2 pieces of lining fabric in
contrasting color, 8½ x 7½
inches (21.6 x 19 cm)

Finished dimensions: 8 x 7¾
inches (20.3 x 19.7 cm)

Seam allowance: ¼ inch
(6 mm)

STITCHES YOU'LL USE

Back stitch

Chain stitch

Satin stitch

Straight stitch (also known
as Running stitch and
Seed stitch)

STENCIL AND STITCH ALONG

1 Size the Catch Up Pouch motif (page 113) to approximately 8 x 6 inches (20.3 x 15.2 cm).

2 Make a copy of the center bird on regular copy paper and cut it out. Trace this onto a piece of cardstock and cut it out with a sharp craft knife to make a stencil. You will be using the negative space opening, so don't worry if the inner shape is destroyed as you remove it. Details that are slightly imperfect will also add to the distressed and primitive mood of the project.

3 Use masking tape to tape the front fabric piece onto a softly padded surface. Use a nonpermanent marker and ruler to make a diagonal line that starts on the left side of the front fabric piece, approximately 3 inches (7.6 cm) up from the bottom edge, and ends on the right side, approximately 1 inch (2.5 cm) up from the bottom edge.

4 Use the diagonal line to guide the stenciling of three birds, placing one entire bird at the center and two partial ones in front and in back. Stencil the bird as follows:
  ▸ Squeeze tiny bits of fabric paint in two shades of green onto a palette and mix slightly. Allow different shades of the green to remain distinct.

▸ Place the stencil onto the fabric at the center so that the front leg of the bird touches the diagonal line.

▸ Hold the stencil with one hand while dipping a stencil brush into the paint and applying it to the fabric within the stencil area.

▸ Remove the stencil.

▸ Repeat to make the bird on the upper left, aligning the rear leg of the bird on the diagonal line.

▸ Repeat to make the third bird on the lower right, aligning the front leg with the diagonal line.

▸ Let the stenciled birds dry.

▸ Add a second diagonal line that runs parallel to the first diagonal line slightly above the top of the birds' wings.

▸ Follow fabric paint manufacturer's instructions to heat-set the piece with a hot iron.

5 Prepare your sewing machine for free-motion stitching by lowering its feed dogs and attaching the darning foot. Thread the machine with black thread. Free-motion-stitch the outlines of the birds and then free-motion stitch little squiggles and lines (freeform, without a transferred motif) in between the three birds and within the two diagonal lines.

6 Remove the piece from the sewing machine and transfer the circle and line portions of the motif (page 113) above and below the birds (see page 10). Secure the fabric in an embroidery hoop and embroider according to the stitch guide.

7 Take the finished piece out of the hoop and remove any transfer lines as needed (see page 12).

8 Make small clusters of satin stitches and straight stitches for the middle and right birds for their eyes and eyelashes. Attach seed beads to the centers with a needle and thread.

SEW ALONG

1 Prepare your sewing machine for standard straight sewing by returning the feed dogs to the original position and attaching the standard sewing foot.

2 Pin one of the top edge strips onto the embroidered piece, right sides facing. Machine-stitch. Open the seam and press. Attach the remaining top edge strip to the backing fabric in the same way.

3 Follow manufacturer's instructions to fuse a piece of fusible webbing to the wrong side of the front piece. Repeat to fuse the remaining piece to the backing fabric. True up the two fused pieces to make sure that they are the same size.

4 Attach the zipper foot to your sewing machine and install the zipper as follows:

▸ With right sides facing, pin the zipper to the top edge of the embroidered piece. Stitch in place, removing pins as you go.

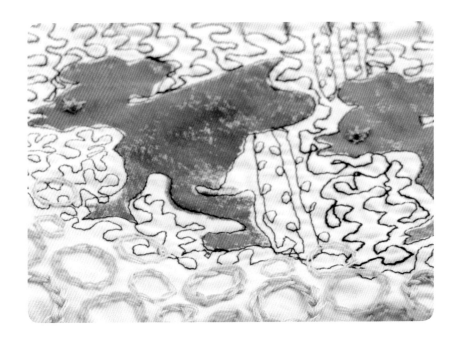

- Pin one of the lining pieces on top, with the right side of the lining facing the wrong side of the zipper. Stitch along the top edge directly over the first stitch line, removing pins as before.
- Press the seam and pull the lining up and over so that wrong sides of the fabrics are facing, and the nonstitched edge of the zipper is at the top.
- Attach the back fabric and lining in the same way to the opposite

side of the zipper, making sure the linings will be facing each other on both side of the zipper when turned right side out. Press as before.

5 Attach the standard foot to your sewing machine and stitch the sides of the bag:
- Place the stitched pouch on your work surface with the zipper in the middle (running top to bottom) and the right sides of the front/ back piece and the linings facing.

- Pin around the edges and open the zipper.
- Stitch on all sides, leaving a 4-inch (10.2 cm) opening on the bottom edge of the lining layers.

6 Turn the bag right side out. Whipstitch the opening closed with a hand-sewing needle and thread. Push the lining into the bag.

Catch Up Pouch Motif

enlarge 200%

variagated
Back Stitch

variagated
Straight Stitch

variagated
Satin Stitch

lime green
Chain Stitch

Jackie Says

- I embroidered some of the circles with six strands of embroidery floss, others with five, four, three, two, and one strand(s).
- I embroidered the lines with the variegated perle cotton.
- I embroidered the eyes with two strands of floss and the eyelashes with the variegated perle cotton.

GATHER UP

Stitching Tool Kit (page 8)

Birds of a Feather Tote motifs (page 117)

1½ yards (1.37 m) of black discharge cotton fabric*

1 sheet of plain white copy paper

Black fine-point marker

1 sheet of compressed rectangular sponge

Shallow dish

Bleach

Rubber gloves

Large piece of plastic (to cover your work surface)

Softly padded work surface: for example, a table
  with a large piece of foam or a stack of newspaper
  or layers of towels

White fabric paint

Foam brush

Sewing machine with darning foot and standard foot

Sewing machine thread: white and black

Perle cotton, 1 skein each of white (size 3 and size 8),
  and red (size 8)

* Discharge fabric is designed to allow its dye to
  become removed in unique and artistically pleasing
  patterns when it comes into contact with bleach or
  other chemicals. Not all fabrics will discharge so
  look for cotton fabric that can discharge or test a
  piece of fabric to see if it will discharge.

Finished dimensions: 16½ x 13 inches
(41.9 x 33 cm)

Seam allowance: ¼ inch (6 mm)

STITCHES YOU'LL USE

Chain stitch

French knot

Birds of a Feather Tote

You are sure to learn many unique methods as you stamp, stitch, and sew this very artistic tote together.

STAMP AND STITCH ALONG

1 Cut the following pieces from the black discharge cotton fabric:

▸ Outer bag and lining
  (cut 2): 33½ x 13½ inches
  (85 x 34.3 cm)

▸ Handles (cut 1): 34 x 7 inches
  (86.4 x 17.8 cm)

▸ Decorative side tabs (cut 1):
  12 x 7 inches (30.5 x 17.8 cm)

2 The motifs (page 117) are shown actual size; approximately 3 x 2 inches (7.6 x 5.1 cm) for the large bird and approximately 2 x 1½ inches (5.1 x 3.8 cm) for the small bird. Enlarge or reduce the motif size as desired.

3 Prepare the compressed sponges:

▸ Make a copy of the motifs on regular copy paper and cut out the center body portions of the birds with scissors.

▸ Use a black fine-point marker to trace the large cutout twice onto the compressed sponge. Trace the small cutout once onto the compressed sponge.

▸ Cut out the traced shapes.

▸ Soak the cutout sponge pieces in water to make them expand. Squeeze out excess water.

4 Pour a small amount of bleach into a shallow dish. Place a piece of plastic to cover and protect your work surface. Wearing rubber gloves, dip the surface of one of the larger sponge cutouts into bleach and then stamp it onto the fabric strip for the handles. The bleach will discolor the fabric, leeching out the back. Repeat for the side tabs and lining piece.

5 With wrong sides facing, fold and press the outer bag fabric in half so that the short sides meet. Open it back up and place it horizontally and right side up onto a padded work surface. The left half of this piece is where you will be stamping and stitching your motif.

6 To make the design shown, plan for:
- ▸ 1 column of 3 small birds on the left side
- ▸ 2 columns of 4 large birds
- ▸ 2 columns of 5 small birds
- ▸ Transfer the large and small bird motifs (see page 10) onto the left-hand half of the outer bag fabric. It is okay for the bird motifs to overlap one another.

7 With a foam brush, lightly dab white fabric paint onto the remaining large sponge cutout. Stamp the image at the center of the first large transferred bird.

Design Note

If you prefer, you can transfer fewer birds. It is also an option to skip the precise transfer of motifs (step 6) and simply stamp the center portion of the birds onto the fabric (step 7). You can then free-motion stitch the tail and face of each bird by eyeballing the design.

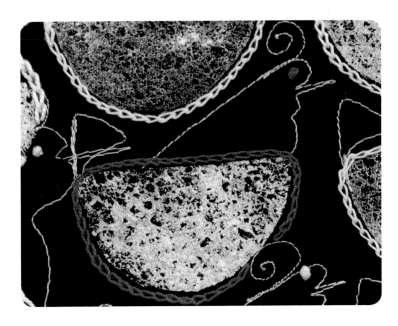

Repeat until the centers of all large birds have been stamped. Use the smaller sponge cutout to stamp the centers of all small birds. Let the paint dry. Follow manufacturer's instructions to heat-set the fabric with a hot iron.

8 Prepare your sewing machine for free-motion stitching by lowering the feed dogs and attaching the darning foot. Thread the machine with white thread. Free-motion-stitch the tail and head section for each bird onto the fabric. Allow the stitching to overlap other birds.

9 Remove the fabric from the sewing machine and place it onto an embroidery hoop. Chain-stitch the center portion of all but one bird with white perle cotton and make French knots for their eyes with white perle cotton. Chain-stitch the one bird with red perle cotton

and make a French knot for the eye with red perle cotton. Take the finished piece from the hoop and remove any transfer lines as needed (see page 12).

SEW ALONG

1 Attach the standard foot to your sewing machine for regular straight sewing with black thread.

2 Press and fold the handles as if making double-fold bias tape:
- ▸ Press the handle fabric strip in half so the long sides meet, wrong sides together.
- ▸ Unfold the strip and press both long sides to the center.
- ▸ Refold on the center fold so the two long side folds are touching; stitch along this edge.
- ▸ Cut the strip in half to make two handles. Turn under all of the short raw ends by ½ inch (1.3 cm) and stitch.

3 Repeat step 2 with the fabric strip for the two side tabs but do not turn under and stitch the short raw ends.

4 Assemble the bag, lining, and tabs:
  ▸ Lay the outer fabric on a clean work surface with the right side facing up and the stamping/embroidery on the left.
  ▸ Place the lining piece on top with right sides facing. Machine-stitch the top long edges of the pieces together. Open up the two pieces and press the seam.

  ▸ Lay the joined pieces flat and fold the entire piece in half with right sides facing, matching the two outer side seams and matching the two lining side seams.
  ▸ Fold and pin the two side tabs in between the side seams of the outer fabric, aligning raw edges of the tabs with the raw edges of the fabric.

5 Stitch the bottom edge of the outer fabric and the sides of both outer fabric and lining, making sure to catch the two tabs and removing pins as you go. Turn the bag right side out.

6 With the lining outside of the bag, turn and press the bottom edges of the lining ½ inch (1.3 cm) to the wrong side, and machine-stitch closed.

7 Push the lining into the bag, leaving approximately ½ inch (1.3 cm) of the lining showing at the top of the bag's edge. Pin the ends of the handles to the inside top edge, about 3½ inches (8.9 cm) from the sides of the bag. Stitch along the top edge of the bag, making sure to add reinforcement stitches where the handles meet the bag.

Birds of a Feather Motifs

shown actual size

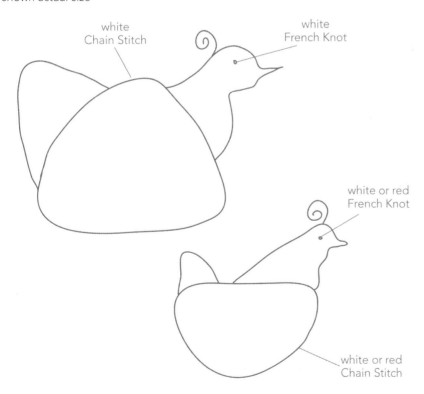

white Chain Stitch

white French Knot

white or red French Knot

white or red Chain Stitch

Jackie Says

  ▸ I used size 3 perle cotton for all of the large birds.
  ▸ I used size 8 perle cotton for all of the small birds.
  ▸ Using two different sized birds and also adding red details to just one bird added a fun and quirky element to the tote.

3 Prepare the white cotton center front piece:

▸ The motif (next page) is shown actual size; approximately 4¾ x 3½ inches (12 x 8.9 cm). Transfer it (see page 10) to the center front piece.

▸ Use an iron set on the hottest setting to press the shiny side of the freezer paper to the wrong side of the center front piece. This will provide stabilization needed for the next two steps.

4 Paint the center front piece as follows. Practice on a scrap piece of fabric first.

▸ Place the center front piece on a flat work surface. Select three or four colors of water-soluble ink blocks and use them to trace lines and lightly fill in small sections of the transferred motif.

▸ Mix one part water and one part textile medium in a shallow dish. Use a small paintbrush to apply the mixture over the traced lines and filled-in sections made with one of the colors of the ink blocks.

▸ Repeat with the other colors, rinsing the paintbrush with water in between color changes. The colors will now intensify and spread and blend slightly.

▸ Allow the image to thoroughly dry. Remove the freezer paper and discard.

▸ Place a thin towel on top of the fabric and press with a hot iron to heat-set.

▸ Trim the fabric to measure 5 x 3 inches (12.7 x 7.6 cm).

5 Add the strips to the center front:

▸ With right sides together, pin one of the 5-inch (12.7 cm) strips onto the bottom long edge of

the center front. Machine-stitch. Press the strip away from the center.

▸ With right sides together, pin the remaining 5-inch (12.7 cm) strip to the right side of the piece. Stitch and press.

▸ Repeat the process with one of the 7-inch (6.4 x 17.8 cm) strips on the top edge of the piece.

▸ Stitch the remaining 7-inch (17.8 cm) strip onto the left side of the piece.

▸ Follow the same process and order to attach the 9-inch (22.9 cm) strips, followed by the 11-inch (27.9 cm) strips.

6 Secure the pieced fabric in an embroidery hoop and embroider according to the stitch guide. Remove the piece from the hoop.

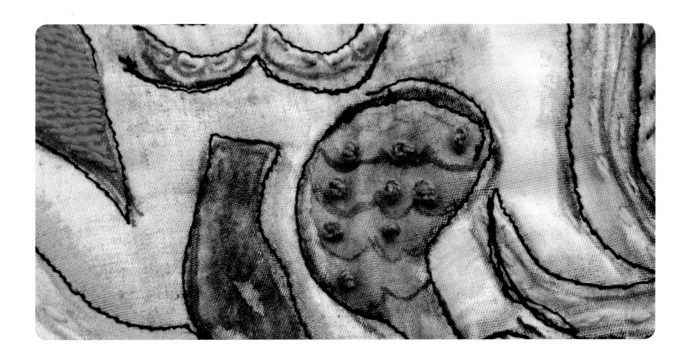

7 Assemble the art quilt:

- Place the backing fabric onto your work surface, wrong side facing up, and spray it with fabric spray adhesive.
- Place the batting on top of the fabric and spray the side of the batting facing you with fabric spray adhesive.
- Place the embroidered piece on top of the batting, right side facing up. The three layers will now be stuck together.
- True up all sides (as needed) so that all thicknesses have the same measurement.

8 Prepare your sewing machine for free-motion stitching by lowering the feed dogs and attaching the darning foot. Free-motion quilt the outline of the bird and some details within the overall motif, being careful not to catch the hand-embroidered stitches.

9 Bind the quilt with the bias binding (see The Ties that Bind, page 13).

Jackie Says

- I used the size 3 perle cotton for the Herringbone stitches on the left side and top edge of the motif.
- For all other stitches, I used size 8 perle cotton.

Dinkie Birdie Art Quilt Motif

shown actual size

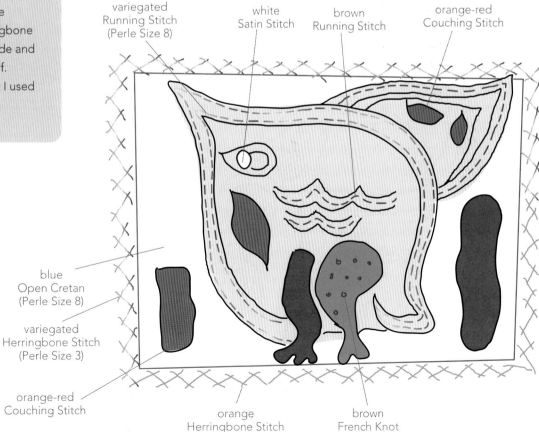

variegated Running Stitch (Perle Size 8)

white Satin Stitch

brown Running Stitch

orange-red Couching Stitch

blue Open Cretan (Perle Size 8)

variegated Herringbone Stitch (Perle Size 3)

orange-red Couching Stitch

orange Herringbone Stitch

brown French Knot

Liesi Cross

id rather be camping

Nicole Vos van Avezathe

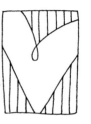

Rebecca Sower

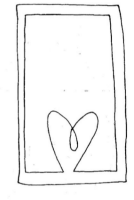

Charlotte Lyons

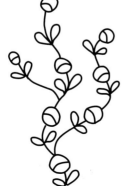

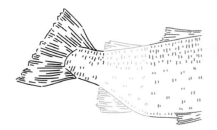

Rainbow Trout

Megan Eckman

Reindeer

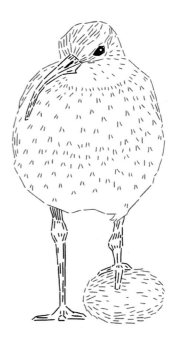

Painted Turtle

Kiwi

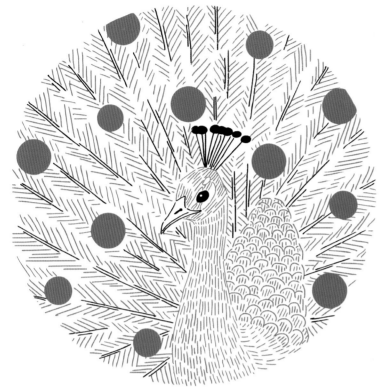

Peacock

Porcupine

Black Crowned Crane

about the *Artists*

To learn more about *Stitch Along*'s contributing artists, visit them here:

Jackie Bowcutt: *www.stitchworks-jackie.blogspot.com*

Liesi Cross: *www.toocrewel.wordpress.com*

Megan Eckman: *www.studiomme.com*

Pam Garrison: *www.pamgarrison.typepad.com*

Carina Envoldsen-Harris: *www.polkaandbloom.com*

Mollie Johanson: *www.wildolive.blogspot.com*

Charlotte Lyons: *www.charlottelyons.com*

Rebecca Sower: *www.rebeccasower.typepad.com*

Sami Teasdale: *www.teasemade.blogspot.com*

Nicole Vos van Avezathe: *www.followthewhitebunny.com*

index

about the author

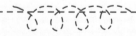

Jenny Doh has authored and packaged numerous books including *Crochet Love, Craft-a-Doodle, Print Collective, Creative Lettering, Stamp It!, Journal It!, We Make Dolls!, Hand in Hand,* and *Signature Styles.* She lives in Santa Ana, California, and loves to create, stay fit, and play music. Visit *www.crescendoh.com.*

Editor: **Beth Sweet**
Technical Editor: **Nancy D. Wood**
Copyeditor: **Amanda Crabtree Weston**
Assistant Editors: **Kerri Winterstein, Monica Mouet**
Designer: **Raquel Joya**
Cover Designer: **Elizabeth Mihaltse**
Photographers: **S. Stills, Jenny Doh**
Model: **Sonia Carey**